Ireland – T

Ireland – The Ducal Days

Michael F. Twist

www.farmingbooksandvideos.com

First Published 2004
by Farming Books and Videos Ltd.

ISBN 1–904871–02–X

A Catalogue Record for this book is available from the British Library

Published by
Farming Books and Videos Ltd.
PO Box 536
Preston PR2 9ZY
Telephone 01772 652693
www.farmingbooksandvideos.com

Front cover photograph: reprinted courtesy of
The Museum of Rural Life, Reading. (The Dairy Shorthorns
in this photograph were not from the Duke's herd.)
Cover design by Pigsty Studios
Edited and set in Baskerville MT by Elizabeth Ferretti
Printed in the UK by Cox & Wyman, Reading

To my dear wife, Cynthia

Contents

Foreword

'Too Rich To Tax' sounds like a flight of fancy, but it is not. When I joined the staff of The Most Noble Hugh Richard Arthur Grosvenor, 2nd Duke of Westminster (Bend Or to his friends) in October 1947 as one of his senior land agents, the Duke was paying nineteen shillings and sixpence in the pound on income tax and surtax. He was without doubt, at that time, the richest man in Great Britain and one of the richest in the world.

Shortly before I joined the Duke, George Ridley, who had worked all his life on the Duke's Eaton Estate, had been appointed agent responsible for this and the extensive Chester housing property. Then on 14 December 1947 the Duke being irritated by Ridley constantly requiring his written authority to conclude contracts and for the disbursement of money, instructed his lawyers to draw up the following document.

> "I, The Most Noble Hugh Richard Arthur, Duke of Westminster DSO hereby state that George Kershaw Ridley of Eaton, Chester, is my duly appointed agent in respect of my estates in England, Wales, Scotland, Ireland and France with authority from time to time to enter into agreements as he may in his absolute discretion deem proper and to perform and do all other acts whatsoever proper to be performed in connection with my estates and affairs generally."

Thus Ridley became responsible, together with his team of helpers, for not only the agricultural estates but also the

Chester and London housing, property and investments. The latter three being subject to approximately eighty per cent death duties, whilst death duties on agricultural investments were fifty-three per cent.

From that day on, until the time of the Duke's death in July 1953, as Ridley put it 'those close to the action' worked tirelessly to keep the inevitable death duties to a minimum, by the *completely legal* use of tax reliefs and 'juggling' of finances. Resulting in a position by February 1953, as recorded at a meeting at the Grosvenor office, where if full legitimate use of tax relief were to be implemented then the richest man in Great Britiain would not be liable for income tax in any form.

Ireland- The Ducal Days is not just about the managment of the Grosvenor millions (now billions) at that time. While the Duke was a most charming and amusing man, he was also autocratic to a degree that at times stretched all members of his staff to the limit of endurance. 'I want' translated into 'I must have, whatever the cost or effect on those involved'. I honestly believe that at times he must have thought himself above the law. He frequently expected senior memebers of his staff to make illegal exchanges of pounds for much-needed dollars, or to smuggle goods from Ireland to England.

This book is full of anecdotes, supported by minutes of meetings, correspondence, newspaper cuttings and photographs. *Ireland – The Ducal Days* is not some flight of fancy, it is an account of what today would seem like a return to a feudal age. In spite of his egotism and apparent lack of concern for those he frequently subjected to strain, working for the Duke is an experience I would not have liked to have missed, although I could have done without a working dinner with Ridley the evening before my wedding!

Michael F. Twist
Woolpit, Suffolk

Extract from Minutes of the Meeting held on 4th February 1953

Minutes of the Meeting held at the Grosvenor Office, 53, Davies Street, London, W.1. on the 3rd and 4th February 1953.

Present:-
Mr G. K. Ridley (in the chair), Mr J. F .S. Saunders, Mr G. I. Barty-King, Mr A. North Hickley, Mr Langshaw Rowland, Col. R. Neilson, Mr M. F. Twist, Mr T. V. H. Coffey, Mr G. Singer, Mr G. S. Beesly, Mr G. J. Reyburn, Mr J. Crocker, Mr I. Donald, Sir Bernard Blatch

Mr Ridley's Statement

Mr Ridley opened the meeting by saying that it was a very important one as we had now reached a stage in our policy when it was necessary to make a fresh assessment of the position. We have achieved all our original intentions in that large sums of money have been invested in agricultural estates and in improvements to them, and in forestry and real estate abroad.

He quoted the Marquis of Downshire's case and suggested it may be possible for the Duke to take similar action.

With the various tax reliefs, to which the Duke was entitled, we had reached a position where he would be entitled to recover all the tax that he paid, and concern was felt as to what might be the result if the Inland Revenue were informed that, in view of this, there would be no tax contributions from the Duke of Westminster for the next few years.

It was decided that Sir Bernard Blatch should consider the possible effects of such a position and, unless there was no real likelihood of legislation being introduced to limit the amount of tax relief available to the Duke, that it would be more diplomatic for the Duke to forego certain tax reliefs to which he was entitled, i.e. on bank interest and by placing new woodlands under Schedule 'B' instead of Schedule 'D'. It was also decided that Mr Langshaw Rowland should look into the possibility of purchasing two new estates of mature timber in Yorkshire and Hampshire, and also the possibility of purchasing devasted areas for immediate replanting.

Annacis Island

Annacis Island was a potential Mayfair in the future of the Grosvenor family, and it is hoped that, if things go according to plan, and by the investment of a certain amount of Trustee money in the development of the Island, there may be future benefits far above what was first anticipated.

Prologue

Being one of the senior land agents to the Most Noble Hugh Richard Arthur Grosvenor, 2nd Duke of Westminster, was not simply a job, it could better be described as an adventure – one I nearly missed. Had that happened I would have been the poorer by the loss of experiences which bordered on the unbelievable, the essence of many being positively feudal. I was participating in a way of life so far removed from that known to the majority of mankind, that, at times, it almost merged into the realms of fantasy. It was to live in a world where 'I want' automatically translated into 'arrange it, whatever the cost, whatever the problems'. I quickly learned that His Grace was not at all receptive to the word 'no' and even less so to 'I don't think that would be possible Your Grace'. Indeed, when you are the wealthiest man in Great Britain, and one of the wealthiest in the world, very little is impossible.

My entrée into the service of the Duke came via cattle. Let me explain. I had for seven years been land agent-cum-farms manager to Colonel Devereux M.F.H., owner of the Roundhill Estate in the Vale of Aylesbury. During that time the Dairy Shorthorn herd maintained on one of the farms had come into prominence. As a result I came to know Henry Hamilton, manager of the Home Farms on the Duke's Eaton estates just outside Chester. The Eaton herd of Dairy Shorthorns was the largest and most famous in the country. There was a further link. The head herdsman at Roundhill, Dick Powley, was the elder brother of the head herdsman at Eaton. Through this connection it became known that I was leaving Colonel Devereux. Conversely, through the same source, I learned that the Duke had purchased a farm at Maynooth in Co. Kildare and proposed moving a small section of his Shorthorn herd to Ireland.

A few weeks before I was to hand over the management of Roundhill, I received a letter from Henry. It was long. It started off by saying he had heard big changes were about to take place at Roundhill. 'Ah,' I thought, 'he's after Dick to go to Ireland.' I had just reached this conclusion when the phone rang – I was urgently required at one of the farms. I put the letter in a drawer of my desk and forgot about it.

Just prior to my leaving the estate, I was putting some papers away and came across the letter. I read it. To my surprise it was not Powley who Henry Hamilton was interested in – it was me! Would I consider going to Ireland to develop the herd and manage the Duke's farm of some 160 acres? The answer was simple – I would not. I had been responsible for nearly 2,000 acres, several pedigree herds, a large stud of hunters, a very big commercial grass-drying enterprise, plus the first ever Artificial Insemination Centre for cattle in the country. In addition, the Old Berkeley West hunt, with which I was very involved, kennelled its foxhounds on the estate.

The post, as suggested by Henry Hamilton, could only be that of a working farm manager-cum-head herdsman, should I take it on it would be a retrograde step. I wrote at once, most politely, saying I was not interested. As an afterthought and very much with tongue in cheek, I added a P.S. – namely, if His Grace required an agent to run all his Irish properties, I knew he had two more much bigger than the Maynooth one, then possibly I might be interested. A few days later I left Roundhill. I departed almost immediately to Mousehole in Cornwall, for a long overdue holiday and some sea fishing. In the seven and a half years I'd been with Colonel Devereux I'd had one short break.

Working for the Colonel was no sinecure, he was a high-powered industrialist and, as such, could normally only visit the estate at weekends. He was a dynamic personality and, if one stayed the course, it was an education working for him, but he did have a few idiosyncrasies. One was that he considered four hours sleep, out of the twenty-four, was quite enough for anyone. This led to him not infrequently calling board meetings of his companies at 6.00am or, in summer time, for the Colonel and me to be riding around the estate of a Sunday morning before the birds were properly awake!

I had been in Cornwall for about three weeks when, returning one evening around 7.00pm from a day's fishing off Land's End with my two longshoreman friends, I found a telegram awaiting me. I was to phone my father immediately – most urgent. This I did. It was to learn that a letter had arrived for me from George Ridley, agent to the Duke. He wished to see me on Saturday at 12.15pm at the Duke's London residence, Bourdon House, on the corner of Davies Street and Berkeley Square. It was Friday, the time by now 7.30pm! The night train, the Cornish Riviera Express, left Penzance around nine o'clock. Hastily I arranged with father to meet me at Reading, the nearest point to my home at which the train stopped, and hung up. Then followed a mad rush to reach the station on time.

The train was already crowded by the time I got there. With difficulty I found a seat – a sleeper was out of the question. After a near-sleepless night, I was beginning to wonder if it would be worth all the hassle. However, breakfast, followed by a good soak in a hot bath, revived me. Having donned my city clothes, dug out my bowler and umbrella, I headed for London.

I arrived at Bourdon House five minutes before the appointed time and was shown into the dining room by the butler. Silently he left, assuring me that he would inform Mr Ridley of my arrival. I looked around the room. So this was how the wealthiest man in the British Isles lived. I sat down and waited, passing the time by trying to calculate the value of the pictures and furnishings. I continued to wait. I began to feel slightly peeved. I had been brought up to believe that time was time. My father, who was also a land agent, was a terror over this. If he had an appointment he would be there five minutes before the stated time. He would remain five minutes after and, if the person he was to meet had not turned up, he would depart, assuming they were not going to show up. I looked at my wristwatch – 12.41pm Should I go? On reflection that did not seem such a good idea, having travelled all night to keep the appointment.

As I cogitated what I should do, the door burst open and a small bespectacled man rushed into the room. Two things struck me immediately – apart from the curvature to his spine – the way he positively exuded vitality, and the shrewdness of the look he gave me. He advanced across the room, hand outstretched, a friendly smile dissolving the hardness I had momentarily glimpsed. Although it is over forty years ago, I can remember the conversation almost verbatim.

"So sorry to keep you, Twist. I'm George Ridley. The Duke left here this morning and there were a number of things he suddenly wanted me to attend to. You know how it is."I did. All resident land agents do.

"Have a drink? I'm having a pink gin."

"Thank you, I'll have the same, not too much pink."

"Best if you fix your own. I gather you know Ikey Bell?"

"Well, it would be untrue to say I know him. I have met him. It's my father who knows him quite well." Ikey Bell, of whom more later, was a famous Master of Hounds and a lifelong friend of the Duke.

"Hmmm. I believe Henry Hamilton has told you all about the Duke's properties in Ireland? Tells me you wouldn't be interested in running just the dairy farm at Maynooth, but might be in being His Grace's agent in Ireland."

"That's correct."

"Yes, well I'll talk to the Duke and let you know."

He glanced at his watch. "I must rush, should just catch the train for Crewe. Finish your drink in peace. Ring the bell when you're ready. Arthur will show you out." He downed the remainder of his drink, shook me by the hand again and was gone. I saw no point in remaining isolated in ducal splendour, so quickly finished what was left in my glass, rang the bell and walked out into the hall. Arthur Wright, whom later I came to know well, ushered me out. I looked at my watch. It was exactly four minutes to one o'clock. I remember wondering if it had really been worth travelling all night and missing a day's fishing for such a cursory interview.

That night I returned to Cornwall. Some two weeks later I received a letter, forwarded from my home. It was from Ridley offering me the post as land agent to His Grace, with the Irish properties as my main priority. If I accepted I was to report to the Eaton estate office at 9.00am on the first Monday in October. So started my association with the 2nd Duke of Westminster.

In passing I should mention that it was not the first time that a member of my family had been connected with the Grosvenors. My paternal grandmother was a Fuller. Her grandfather, Henry Fuller, had been physician to the Earl of Grosvenor in the early part of the nineteenth century, having succeeded his father, Dr John Fuller, in a practice which the latter had commenced around 1776. By the time Henry joined his father they had a monopoly amongst the notable residents of Mayfair. So much was this the case that Henry Fuller would refuse to visit a patient who moved north of Oxford Street 'as being too distant for attendance'. Dr Henry appears to have been quite a character and an amusing reference to him can be found in *Leaves from the Note Books of Lady Dorothy Nevill* (Macmillan & Co. 1907)

Lady Dorothy writes: 'The ways and things of the sixties seem very strange today. The hideous crinoline was universally worn by ladies and entailed untold inconvenience and discomfort. Old Dr Fuller of Piccadilly was once summoned to dislodge a fish-bone from the throat of Frances Anne, Lady Londonderry, and when imperiously told to begin, was obliged to say that he was quite unable to get within many yards of her ladyship's throat in consequence of her crinoline being so enormous and solid.'

Henry Fuller was a keen shot and on excellent terms with Earl Grosvenor, whom he frequently accompanied on shooting expeditions. The doctor recorded how, when on his way to join the Earl around 1818, he flushed a covey of partridges, happily dusting themselves in Berkeley Square, 'so near was the district to open fields'. He goes on to tell how he and the Earl used to go for a few hours' snipe and duck shooting over marshlands, now built over and forming part of Pimlico and Belgravia.

Apparently the marshes were 'reclaimed' and converted into possible building land through the foresight of Earl Grosvenor when he permitted thousands of tons of soil, excavated in the making of the London Docks, to be dumped on them. This much to the annoyance and frustration of the good doctor, who felt forced to point out to his friend that the marshes were much the best snipe and duck shooting that could be found within easy reach of the City!

Three books have already been written about the 2nd Duke of Westminster, the legendary Bend Or. They cover the family history, the Duke's quite outstanding achievements as a soldier in both the Boer War and the First World War and, inevitably, they record his marriages and mistresses. There is no room for another along such lines. Therefore, much of the following will be confined to how the Grosvenor millions, now billions, were saved from crippling death duties. Further, it is intended to record many anecdotes regarding this remarkable man from my own experiences, together with a number related to me by Ikey Bell, Major Basil Kerr, many years land agent at Eaton, and George Ridley. It was the latter who did more than any other person to ensure the continuation of the Grosvenors' legendary wealth.

1
A Cursory Interview

I arrived at Chester around 5.30pm on the first Sunday in October 1947. It had been a long tiring drive from South Bucks in a somewhat clapped-out Ford Prefect – quite literally the only car I could buy. Cars were at a premium after the war and the one I had had at Roundhill belonged to the Colonel. I had been booked in at the Talbot Hotel, where bed and breakfast was to be provided, paid for by the estate. I was greeted by the manager, who seemed to know who I was, for he immediately began to extol the virtues of the Duke. But then why shouldn't he? His Grace owned the hotel, as he did much of Chester. Having unpacked and settled into my room, I made my way downstairs and sought someone to find out how I got to Eccleston, one of the many villages on the Eaton estates and owned by the Duke. The only person around proved to be the manager, who quickly answered my queries and enquired if I would like a drink. The answer was in the affirmative.

Having refreshed myself, I got into the car and headed out across the bridge over the River Dee. Once I had achieved this it was all straight forward. On the outskirts of Eccleston village I spotted an imposing looking house, only partly visible from the road. It appeared to have gothic towers, vaguely I seemed to remember a feature of Eaton Hall. Could this ornate building be the Duke's residence? How wrong can one be? This impressive structure was merely the agent's house – the home of Major Basil Kerr, by then retired and whose term of office as land agent at Eaton had spanned thirty-four years.

The Major had a delightful personality, great charm and an endless fund of stories, many about 'The Owner' – a name frequently used by members of the staff when talking about the Duke. After a couple of most enjoyable hours in his company, during my early days at Eaton, I came to the conclusion that probably he hadn't been a particularly brilliant land agent. However, one thing was patently obvious, he had been endowed with two great gifts – common sense and unlimited charm. He had another great attribute – the ability to delegate and leave the person concerned to get on with the job. I was to learn, in due course, that he was very much the confidant of the Duke – truly a power within the ducal realm!

I continued on into the park and quickly discovered the estate office and the stud. It was a nice evening and so I decided to continue a little further. Suddenly I had my first view of Eaton Hall, not improved by a host of army huts in front of it. The main building had been given over to the army during the war, only the private wing being retained by the Duke. I got out of the car, leaned on the roof and gazed. I wasn't really impressed – I'd never seen anything quite like it before. It seemed to be all bits and pieces, with gothic towers sprouting from it like an unruly crop of mushrooms. The most imposing thing was the clock tower, which quite rightly, I discovered later, reminded me of Big Ben.

This architectural oddity was the brainchild of one Alfred Waterhouse, who had been commissioned by the first Duke to redesign and rebuild the hall. Up to that time Waterhouse's claim to fame, if any, was that he had been the architect responsible for the Natural History Museum in Kensington, and the Town Hall in Manchester. When completed, many of the nobility considered the latest Grosvenor extravaganza to be in the worst possible taste. However, that apparently did not worry the Duke. He liked it, and that was all that mattered.

Dick Powley's wife (Dick's father had for years been head herdsman at the Home Farm) told me that as a girl she had worked as a housemaid at The Hall – every bedroom had a fireplace, as did most of the bathrooms! Truly a strange building, which was shortly to be demolished, but oh so much more preferable to that which replaced it. I only saw the latter once, when staying with my friend Henry Hamilton, years after I had ceased to have anything to do with the Westminster estates. It reminded me of something that might well have 'sprouted' beside a motorway! The fifth Duke was, I believe, responsible for the current Eaton Hall. One can only think that when he authorized its building he had internal comfort foremost in his thoughts, rather than architectural beauty!

The following morning I arrived at the estate office just before nine o'clock. I made my way up the stairs to 'reception' and introduced myself. I was informed that Mr Ridley would see me immediately and I was ushered into his office, a pleasant room. George Ridley beamed at me across a vast desk and bade me welcome. I remember thinking what a huge desk for a comparatively small man. However, I was quickly to learn that he might well be smallish in stature, but whatever he lacked in this sphere he more than made up for in mental ability. He told me that whilst at Eaton I could use the Stud Room, on the ground floor, as an office. He then took me to meet the staff, finishing up where I had started – at reception – where he introduced me to the young lady to whom I had first spoken, Mrs Potter. He went on to say that she would type any letters I might require doing, and generally look after my needs. Then with a chuckle added, "Strictly from a secretarial point of view."

He instructed her to look out all the Irish files and take them down to my temporary office. This was a rather cheerless room, sparsely furnished, but it too sported a mammoth-sized desk. The walls were unadorned, except for a case containing the racing-silks worn by that great jockey Fred Archer when riding for the 1st Duke. The latter, who was totally immersed in the management and well-being of his racehorses and stud, achieved the unique distinction of being the only person ever to twice breed and race the winner of the Triple Crown – the 2000 Guineas, the Derby and the St Leger. During the time he was involved in racing, the 1st Duke won something in excess of 340 races to a value of more than 300,000 guineas. A sum that these days would be considered 'chicken feed' in the bloodstock world, but at the time was a vast fortune.

There seems little doubt that, of the many winners the 1st Duke owned, Bend Or was his favourite. When he was presented with a grandson, Hugh Richard Arthur (he already had two granddaughters) he almost immediately gave the babe the sobriquet Bend Or, after his famous and noted stallion. Over the years, as I learned more and more about the 2nd Duke's many amours, I sometimes wondered if he had felt that, having been given the agnomen of such a noted stallion, he had something to live up to – certainly, in modern parlance, as a young man he was a noted stud! I well remember his eldest daughter, Lady Ursula, saying to me one evening while in the throes of one of her not infrequent feuds with her father which, if I remember rightly, had something to do with the current Duchess, and I was trying to pour oil on troubled waters.

"Michael, the trouble with my father is, that when he was a young man, he could never keep his flies done up and it seems he still can't."

She gazed at me with soft limpid eyes, which I had come to realise was a sign that, even with her quite phenomenal capacity, she'd had more than enough gin! Over the years I came to know Ursie well, liked her tremendously, unlike a number of my colleagues. However, during any business dealings with her, I always kept my kid gloves handy – she could be quite vitriolic, particularly if she was discussing George Ridley, for whom she never showed any great love!

I settled down to read the files. The only one which bore a name that meant anything to me was the one labelled 'Isaac Bell Esq.' – Ikey. It would be appropriate at this point to say a little about this great character, known to thousands and loved by hundreds in the world of fox hunting. Ikey was an American, although he spent virtually his entire life in England and Southern Ireland. He was educated at Harrow and Cambridge, but only lasted a few terms at the latter. As he once explained to me with great solemnity – he found study interfered with his fox hunting. There just wasn't time for both so he felt, quite naturally, the former had to go!

He first met the Duke when he was still at Harrow and the young Duke was at Eton. The schools had a fixture for a soccer match, which was abandoned due to really terrible weather. Whilst waiting for it to improve the two teams passed the time in various forms of 'horseplay', bringing Ikey and Bend Or together. As a result a deep friendship began between them that lasted their lifetime.

Ikey was a nephew of the great American newspaper tycoon, Gordon Bennett, owner of one of New York's most prestigious and profitable daily papers. Ikey, not once, but many times, told me that when he was twenty-one his uncle gave him the opportunity either of joining him in the business and becoming his sole heir or, his uncle told him, he could have sufficient capital in dollars to give him an income equivalent to £25,000 to £30,000 per annum – this at the end of the nineteenth century was phenomenal wealth, indeed beyond the dreams of avarice! Ikey told me he had no difficult in opting for the latter and immediately set about realising his greatest ambition – to become a Master of Foxhounds.

He soon, even at an early age, became one of the best-known personalities in the hunting world. He was, in this sphere, to become one of those rare phenomena – a legend in his own lifetime. His knowledge of foxhound breeding put him on the same level as the greatest authorities on this subject. He was a brilliant amateur huntsman, fearless horseman, and he carried the horn with three famous packs of which he was Master – the Galway Blazers, the Kilkenny and the South and West Wilts.

Sadly, by the time I got to know Ikey he was on crutches, but through sheer grit and bloody-minded determination 'to prove the quacks wrong', he eventually walked with two sticks – one of which I have, given to me by that great man not long before he died. His debilitating lameness was generally believed to have been caused by a hunting accident. However, he assured me on more than one occasion that it had been due to a stupid prank.

He and a number of chums had dined and wined well. One of the party suggested they have a jumping competition and built 'a fence' with the dining-room chairs. Ikey was the first to go, cheered on by his friends. He took on the formidable obstacle and crashed to the floor. Although the lasting effects were not immediately apparent and he did, subsequently, take a terrible fall out hunting; he always laid the blame for his immobility to the fact that he wasn't as good a jumper as his horses! If that wasn't enough, in December 1946 he had a major operation for cancer and was given only three to six months at the most to live – I went to his funeral in the mid sixties! He was an incredibly generous man to his friends, none more so than to his dear friend and idol – Bend Or.

I sat in my rather gloomy 'office' going through the files, reading copies of numerous letters to people whom I had never heard of and really very little made sense except George McVeagh's file. He was a solicitor in Dublin, who in the years to come, became one of my closest friends. In due course I was to learn from the deed boxes, neatly stacked on shelves along one wall of his office, that George was well connected. Amongst those whose names appeared were the Aga Khan, who had extensive interests in bloodstock in Ireland, a number of knights, baronets and at least three Embassies, but pride of place went to the Duke!

George, I was to learn, was no legal genius. His strength was threefold. First, no task was too great. Secondly, he, like the Duke, did not know the meaning of the word 'no'. Thirdly – and undoubtedly his greatest asset – he knew everyone who was anyone in Ireland, from the Taoiseach (the Prime Minister) downwards! Those he didn't know knew him, for he was a great athlete, representing his country many times at cricket, tennis, squash and hockey. Any task, great or small, was approached with the same energy and enthusiasm which he displayed as he flew down the wing in a hockey international! Life, as far as George was concerned, was for living.

Not long after he became the Duke's Irish solicitor, McVeagh was due to go to Sweden with the Irish Davis Cup Team, of which he was captain. It was typical that he wrote to the Duke informing him of this fact and asking if the latter could give him any introductions in Sweden. George Ridley was staying at the Duke's Irish residence at the time. When he'd read the letter 'The Owner' turned to Ridley and said, "McVeagh wants an introduction in Sweden. Only person I know is the King. Think that'll do?" George told me that he'd replied in the affirmative. "Right, I'll send a telegram." It read something as follows.

> "My friend McVeagh, captain Irish Davis Cup team, visiting your country. Grateful if you would show him hospitality. Westminster."

He handed it to Ridley. "Get this sent off for me."

George had taken the slip of paper and enquired, "Where shall I send it?"

The reply came back rather tersely, "Oh, to the King of Sweden, Oslo, I suppose."

George had smiled and pointed out that Oslo was in Norway.

The Duke, obviously somewhat peeved, immediately replied, "What's it matter? All these buggers know each other."

The King of Sweden, himself a keen tennis player,

sought out George and the other Irish players and invited them to the palace. They played a hard-fought men's doubles – George partnering His Majesty. The latter, who was getting on in years, made it very clear to his opponents that he wanted no royal prerogative and no quarter shown. George and his partner won. (Alas, Ireland lost their round of the Davis Cup!) After play had finished, George lunched with the King. A photograph of George being partnered by His Majesty took pride of place on George's desk for many years.

I finished reading the files, sat back and looked at my watch – it was just 10.35am I had taken less than two hours to bone up on my new job. The trouble was, having read the files, I wasn't that much wiser. I had discovered that the Duke's residence in Ireland was Fort William, Lismore, Co. Waterford, and that it adjoined the Lismore Castle Estates, the property of the Duke of Devonshire. I also discovered that 'The Owner' had a stud farm at Bruree in Co. Limerick. It was managed by Major Stephen Vernon, the Duke's son-in-law. who was married to Lady Ursula, the Duke's eldest daughter.

Lady Ursula had previously been married to William Patrick Filmer-Sankey, formerly of the First Life Guards. Described to me some years later by Basil Kerr as 'a bit of a bounder'. The Major had then embarked on an intriguing if, I thought, a somewhat improbable story.

Soon after Ursula married she and her first husband were invited to Eaton, the latter to be one of the guns at the first big pheasant shoot of the season, for which Eaton was famous. In the early hours of the morning on the day of the shoot, Basil Kerr claimed he was aroused by a frightful commotion outside his house. On going to investigate he found two of the gamekeepers with a poacher – none other than the Duke's son-in-law! When asked what the hell was going one, the latter had immediately replied, "Knocking off a few pheasants, so as to get some money to tip the keepers at the end of the day!" I gathered from Major Kerr that once 'The Owner' got to hear about the incident, William Patrick was definitely *persona non grata* at Eaton Hall. I once asked Ikey Bell if the story was true. He replied without hesitation.

"Wouldn't doubt it for a minute, the chap was a rotter, never could stand the fellow. Anyway why should Basil make up a story like that? He'd enough, if he cared to tell them, to fill a library."

I was checking a long list of questions I had made to ask Ridley, when the door opened and he entered.

"All right?"

"Yes thanks, but I've a host of queries."

"I'm sure you have, in fact I'd be very concerned if you hadn't. You can't take it all in at once. I have to go into Chester now, but I'll pick you up soon after two o'clock, show you part of the estate and we can have a good talk then."

With that he was gone.

I'd just started to read McVeagh's file again, when there was a tap on the door and a cheerful looking man entered. "Ah! You're alone. I'm Bill Bryan."

I stood up, hand outstretched. "Delighted to meet you. Who are you and where do you fit in?" Bill laughed and dropped into a chair.

"Me? I'm George Ridley's cousin – trust him not to mention my existence. I act as secretary, I suppose you could call it that, to the Duke. I'm an accountant really, had my own business before the war. If you've time to spare I'll try and put you in the picture over Ireland. That is if you'd like me to?"

"I've all the morning and I most certainly would like."

Bill pulled out a cigarette case, offered me one, lit up and settled back in his chair. It transpired that the Duke had gone to Ireland to visit his old friend Ikey Bell. Their travels took them to Cork and they booked in at one of its best hotels. The latter was not at all to the Duke's liking and he had proceeded to browbeat Ikey and tell him it was all his fault. Further, he told his friend that he better find them somewhere different to stay. Hadn't he any friends in the neighbourhood?

Relating the incident to me, some years later, Ikey assured me that the Duke had got himself in a right paddy. The only people Ikey knew within the area were General and Mrs Sullivan of Glanmire, just outside Cork. Ikey phoned the General. Could he bring the Duke of Westminster to stay for a night or two? To begin with the answer was an emphatic 'no'. The General claimed he was not in the position to entertain someone like Westminster, but, Ikey assuring him that Bend Or was no different from anyone else, eventually won the day. Within the hour the party had arrived at Glanmire. Bill stubbed out his cigarette and grinned.

"That was that!"

"Sorry, I don't follow."

He went on to explain that Anne Sullivan (better known as Nancy), the General's daughter, had just returned home having been away serving with the FANY (First Aid Nursing Yeomanry) since the early days of the war. It was, Bill assured me, a case of 'love at first sight'. When the Duke returned to England, he came straight to Eaton and sent for Ridley. The latter was to go to Ireland at once and buy him a house, with land, within easy distance of Cork, in other words Glanmire. Further, he was to buy a stud farm, also in the south of the country, and a dairy farm near Dublin.

Bill laughed, "Cousin George really had to get his skates on, for the Duke wanted the house as of yesterday. He was hardly given time to pack a bag." However, let me continue the saga. Ridley crossed on the ferry from Holyhead to Dún Laoghaire and joined Ikey at the Shelbourne Hotel in Dublin. Ikey immediately introduced Ridley to George McVeagh and the latter, with his customary speed, quickly had details of a number of properties for the Duke's envoy to inspect. It had been made very clear to McVeagh that at this stage no mention of the Duke was to be made, in case it caused an escalation in property prices!

In the shortest possible time, George Ridley hired a chauffeur-driven limousine and set off, together with Ikey, in search of the required properties. George had instructions to report daily progress to 'The Owner'. Ikey managed to waste quite a few hours by taking Ridley to see a number of properties owned by friends and acquaintances. Charming relics of the past, requiring months of work to restore them to the ducal splendour that was required, from whence to woo Miss Sullivan.

When the Duke had been touring with Ikey, they had visited Lismore. The latter was very anxious he should see a property adjoining the Lismore Castle Estate – owned by the Duke of Devonshire. At the time the castle was unoccupied, but until a few months before it had been the home of Lord Charles Cavendish's widow, previously Adele Astaire, sister to the tap-dancing Fred. Lady Cavendish, I was to learn later, was not popular in Lismore, being frequently referred to as 'the Dripping Duchess'.

Apparently, when touring the kitchen quarters of the castle she had spied a number of bowls of dripping lined up on a shelf. She had asked the cook what happened to so much dripping? The cook had explained that it was part of her perks and she sold it at either sixpence or one shilling a bowl, according to the size, to the villagers. "Not any more," had come the reply. "Sell them at ninepence and one shilling and sixpence and the money is to go into the household account." Adele was not popular. I was told that by nightfall her ladyship had been dubbed 'the Dripping Duchess', a nickname she was never to lose!

Ikey and Ridley arrived at the Lismore property on the Sunday morning, having first contacted the owner, a Mr Dunne. The house was in good repair, magnificently situated overlooking the River Blackwater and had approximately

160 acres that belonged to it. As is customary in Ireland, the deal could not be rushed, but deal there had to be, for Ridley felt certain he could not better the house. At last a price was agreed – £8,000. A further £2,000 was eventually considered by both parties to be an equable amount for what furniture and fittings there were, plus the farm machinery and a small herd of pedigree Hereford cattle.

Highly elated by the thought that his great friend would be coming to live in Ireland, Ikey returned to Dublin, whilst George Ridley went off in search of a stud farm. This he found in Co. Limerick – the Bruree Stud. The house left something to be desired, but had potential. Some 470 acres were included, together with a number of cottages. These days it seems quite unbelievable that such a property could have been bought for £14,000!

Well pleased with himself, George Ridley headed back to Dublin, where he started the ball rolling in his search for a dairy farm. He then returned to England. It was nearly the end of November. 'The Owner' was delighted and could barely wait for the contracts to be exchanged and the purchase completed. Thanks to McVeagh the latter was achieved in record time. Once this happened, Ridley told me in years to come, the Duke was like a small child wanting to play with a new toy. He just couldn't wait to get to Ireland.

It was by then nearly Christmas and His Grace told his Agent that he wished to be in the Fort early in the New Year. Further, that immediately the holiday was over, the latter was to go to Ireland and arrange it. Alas, poor George did not go to Ireland, he went to bed with a very bad bout of influenza!

The Duke was not a happy man. Frustrated in his desires he ordered his secretary, normally based in London, to go to Eire and attend to the job. The latter grudgingly complied with his instructions, only to return within the minimum of time to say it was quite impossible to obtain staff and it could well be months before Fort William could be made habitable. Not a good move! As I have said, His Grace was not really conversant with the word 'no', and most certainly did not like being thwarted in his wishes. Bill stopped and smiled.

"That, as our American buddies would say, was when the shit hit the fan! By the way, what are you doing for lunch?"

"Nothing."

"Right, let's go over to my house, have a G & T. You can meet Betty, my wife, and I'm sure she can find enough for you as well for lunch."

Ten minutes later I was comfortably seated in the drawing room of Bill's small but charming house. He continued the saga.

George Ridley, still in bed and feeling as low as only 'flu can make one, had a visit from the luckless secretary, who in turn had been visiting the Duke. Mr Ridley was to take over the control of all the Duke's personal staff. He protested loud and long that he didn't want the job, but to no avail. The secretary said it had been decreed by His Grace and as far as he, the secretary, was concerned that was the end of the matter. Poor Ridley was furious. He was employed to look after the Eaton Estates, a big job on its own, and he'd already had the Irish venture added to his workload.

Still seething, and no doubt temperature rising, he received a message to say the Duke was coming to see him. Ridley sent one back saying he would visit the Duke and struggled out of bed. When he joined the latter he was given an ultimatum – Fort William had to be ready for occupation by 23 January at the very latest. Further, he told his agent that, from that moment onwards, he was to oversee the personal staff.

George felt too ill to argue. He asked if he might take his cousin, Bill Bryan, to help. He explained that Bill was a Lieutenant Commander in the navy and was at present on leave, staying with him at Eccleston. The Duke had replied that he couldn't care less who he took with him – just as long as the job was done within the stipulated time.

Bill topped my glass up, lit another cigarette, and continued. As soon as Ridley had partially recovered, he, Bill and Richard Chapman, one of the butlers, who eventually became Steward of the Household, set off for Ireland. One of the first problems that confronted the party was where to stay. Good hotels in Ireland, in those days, were a rarity outside the major cities. They opted for the Cahir House Hotel, in the town of that name, about forty minutes drive or less from Lismore.

The hotel was managed, on behalf of her family, by Eileen McCool. She and her brothers, who had the Cahir Garage, proved to be a tremendous help in many spheres in the years that followed. Whilst I would not, in those days, have considered the hotel worthy of an AA rating, it had a very good pointer as to its simple and clean standard of excellence – it was regularly patronized by the priesthood! Having set up headquarters, George's next move was to contact Captain Gerald FitzGerald – part-time land agent for the Duke of Devonshire.

Fitz, as he was invariably known, was only too willing to co-operate. He saw possibilities for himself; also he had no great love for Lady Cavendish, who had returned to America to live. His local knowledge and contacts were invaluable to George Ridley; further there were a number of experienced staff at the Castle, doing virtually nothing. Fitz, when the matter was put to him, could see no good reason for retaining them. It was obvious; they should leave the employ of one Duke for another! There was only one snag. All those employed at the Castle had to give a month's notice, which meant it would be well into February before they could take up new jobs.

This, to George Ridley, seemed totally reasonable. He was very chuffed with himself for having overcome the insuperable, for really experienced house staff were at a premium in Ireland. He wired the good news to the Duke, explaining the situation and asking for a further two weeks in which to complete his allotted task. The reply was both terse and autocratic and was to the effect that all was to be ready by the 23rd and no excuses would be tolerated!

Furious at such a lack of understanding, yet stimulated by both the challenge and the rebuff, George really showed his resourcefulness. It is virtually certain that what he achieved in the early days of 1946, led to the Duke's complete trust in his employee, which in turn gave George Ridley the opportunity to save the major part of the Grosvenor fortune from what would have been crippling death duties, but that was all in the future.

Determined to succeed in his Herculean task Ridley, together with his helpers, rushed back to Dublin to the Shelbourne Hotel. Here the head receptionist was charmed into assisting. This led to the 'borrowing' of the chef from the Clarence Hotel in Dublin – to fill the gap until the cook could leave Lismore Castle to take up her new post. It also brought about the sudden transfer of several maids, again 'on loan', from the Great Northern Hotel at Bundoran to Lismore.

The staff problem was solved. All was organised. But a house fully staffed was no good without furniture, glass, and silver *et cetera*. Back the trio rushed to Eaton, leaving Fitz in temporary command of the Fort. A vast quantity of all that was required was in store at Eaton, having been moved out of The Hall when the army moved in. Bill paused and looked at me.

"Do you know, we were given pretty much a free hand except 'The Owner' decided he wanted a certain huge great crystal chandelier suspended in the main hall at Fort William. To ship it over it had to be completely dismantled, then put together again on arrival! There was something over fifteen hundred pieces." Bill grimaced. "I've never liked chandeliers since."

All was selected, packed in containers and sent on its way. McVeagh had all the paperwork in hand, everything appeared to be under control – then the Irish Customs threw a spanner in the works. They would not release the containers until they had a guarantee that the Duke would not part with any of the imports for at least six months.

A verbal assurance or, indeed, a written one, was not enough. They demanded that a cheque should be deposited with them for a sum roughly three times the value of the goods. Fuming, George Ridley wrote the required cheque and handed it over to McVeagh, who was in charge of the negotiations with the authorities, thinking all would now be well. Not a bit of it! How could the Customs be sure that the Duke had the money to meet the cheque should the occasion arise? Back McVeagh came – the cheque had to be guaranteed by the bank. This was done, and the cheque was accepted.

At last it seemed as though the show could get on the road. A positive cavalcade left Dublin for Fort William. George Ridley told me he almost wept with relief, but the test of his stamina was not yet over – there was further red tape to come! The Dublin Customs told McVeagh that it would be necessary for a customs officer to be at Fort William to see that the containers were still sealed on arrival and to officially break the seals!

George McVeagh really went to town. He sent his assistant by car, through the night to go and fetch the nearest officer who was located in Lismore, and almost hijacked the poor man in the early hours of the morning. While enacting the 'opening ceremony' he was not a very happy man. However, Bill assured me, that when he left he was in fine fettle having thoroughly enjoyed the best of hospitality!

The days that followed were hectic. Bill told me it took him and a band of helpers the best part of a day and well into the night to reassemble the 'bloody chandelier'. Further, a builder had to be employed – Sisks of Cork – to strengthen the ceiling and hang the wretched thing. But, of course, all eventually was well and Sisks did a great deal of work both at Lismore and at the dairy farm at Maynooth in the months to come.

At last all was ready, but only just. The Duke could contain himself no longer and arrived a day early! Richard Chapman by then had the staff 'eating out of his hand', the house well provisioned and an excellent cellar laid down. His Grace arrived to all the comforts that he would normally have expected at Eaton or Bourdon House.

Bill smiled.

"There you are – the story of an Irish miracle."

There is little doubt that Cousin George's achievements in setting up 'the love nest' led to him being in the position of power that he is today, and so obviously being trusted by 'The Owner'. Oh yes, there was one final incident. Do you know that our esteemed employer actually told George off for paying the chef too much – said he wasn't sure he could afford it!

2
I Meet the Duke

It was about twenty minutes past two, when I walked out of the estate office with George Ridley. I looked at the row of cars, wondering which was his. There seemed to be nothing there comparable with the position he held. He walked to a vast, square-built, ancient-looking car – I think it was a Morris Oxford. It was even older than my Ford Prefect! He must have seen the look on my face and laughed.

"It's one of the Duke's cast-offs. I could have had a nice new shooting brake, but I don't wish to appear ostentatious. I don't want people to think George Ridley has changed or, indeed, is changing. I want to remain as I always have."

But he didn't. It was not many years before he had a seat on the board of W Watson (Liverpool) Motor Distributors, largely to advise over tax matters, and was driving a Bentley! And who could blame him? It would be hard to say which was George's greatest attribute, but, if I was put in a position of having to name one, I think I would have to say his extraordinary ability for spotting loopholes in tax laws.

We climbed in and set off. George talked and talked. It was obvious that his life revolved around the Eaton Estates and the Duke – although, on reflection, I think I have these in the wrong order! At last he stopped.

"Tell me Mr Ridley, how long have you been connected with the estate?"

"You can drop the mister, call me George. The answer to your question is ever since I left school. I was very 'chesty' as a youngster and the doctor recommended I should lead an outdoor life. My father, who was in Insurance, knew the head forester here on the estate, Sandy Myles, who agreed to take me on. I worked outside to start with, helping to fell trees, cleaning up woodland, even sweeping leaves on the drives!" He laughed.

"The shoot came under the Forestry Department and suddenly I found myself with a most unusual job. In the late spring and early summer I had to be out on the pheasant-rearing field by dawn. My job was to count and record the number of chicks, as they were let out of the coops every morning. I must have counted more pheasants than any living man. However, it was to have its reward. Sandy Myles decided I was useful at figures and transferred me to the timber yard. From then on I spent a large part of my time measuring up and cubing timber. In January 1931 Major Kerr asked Myles if he knew a young man who was good at figures. The reply was – only young Ridley."

"Right, send him up to the estate office"

Not knowing what was in store for him, or what possible crime he could have committed that necessitated being called to 'head office', young George cycled over to Eccleston. He was ushered in to Basil Kerr almost immediately. What followed is so well chronicled in George Ridley's most excellent book, *Bend Or, Duke of Westminster*, that I can do no better than to quote from it. But first a word about the book. Yes, it is excellent, but in my opinion, not wholly accurate.

Ridley implies that it was the Duke who masterminded the various schemes of financial genius and manipulation, which saved millions in death duties. From where I sat this was not so, and I sat in on many meetings of senior staff and advisers at which ways of saving the family fortune were the main topic of conversation. These conferences usually lasted two days. I not infrequently, at the close of the meeting, saw Ridley give a wry smile and say, "Thank you, gentlemen. Now I've got the hard part to do – selling our proposals to the Duke."

In July 1988 I wrote to George saying how much I had enjoyed his book and what memories it had brought back. Further, that I was surprised that he had given the credit for so many of his innovations to the Duke. He replied on 5 August 1988 as follows:-

Dear Michael,

Thank you for your very kind letter.
Several people who, like you, were close to the action wrote in a similar vein. As you say it was me that thought out the plans and had the task of implemen ting them with the aid of an excellent team, but I do not know of anyone who would have given me such authority as he did.

His successors in title would not have been so brave or imaginative as he was.

Best wishes,

Yours ever,

George

A modest man? No, I don't think so; just one with an incredible sense of loyalty to his friend Benny (Bend Or), to whom George was forever grateful for having given him the opportunity to prove his ability.

To return to 1931 and Ridley's summons to the estate office, I quote in his own words the conversation that took place after he was ushered into Basil Kerr's room.

"Do you know anything about property?"

"No, sir."

"You don't know anything about shops, offices, and residential property?"

"No, sir."

"Do you know anything about rates and taxes?"

"No, sir."

"Do you know anything about building construction?"

"No, sir."

"You'll do, I want you to start next Monday and take over the Chester Estate."

The sub-agent, who managed the property, had died a few weeks earlier. George, delighted with his promotion, set about his task with a great will to succeed. He told me that in a comparatively short space of time he had almost doubled the Chester rental. Well pleased with his achievements, he brought them to the attention of Basil Kerr and suggested a small increase in salary would not be inappropriate. He didn't get an increase, but he did nearly get the sack for having the temerity to make such a suggestion! It appeared that it was not the done thing to ask for a raise in ducal circles! Some long serving member of the staff, I forget who, told me that a footman at Eaton Hall had once had the gall to waylay the Duke and ask for an increase in wages. He was summarily dismissed, packed and gone within the hour! And yet the Duke's generosity to both friends and tenants was, at times, quite staggering.

During my tour I asked carefully worded questions about both the Duke and Duchess. My companion became most eloquent on the subject of the latter. He told me he believed that the Duke had never been happier. He related how Bend Or had continued his courtship of Miss Sullivan throughout 1946. Something that was not entirely popular with her parents, according to Ikey Bell, for he was born in 1879, she in 1915 – a difference of some 36 years between their ages. Eventually he persuaded Nancy to agree to marry him, once he had obtained a divorce from Loelia, the third Duchess, from whom he'd been separated for a number of years. The divorce became absolute in January 1947.

By 7 February they were married. The ceremony took place at the Chester Registry Office and again, George Ridley was closely involved. It was he who was instructed to make all the arrangements and acted as a witness, together with the new Duchess's brother – George Sullivan. The fact that her parents were not present is an indication that perhaps Ikey's surmise was correct.

The knot being securely tied, one might be forgiven in

thinking that, at last, the agent's job was complete. But no, his next task was to hold a press conference and hoodwink the press into thinking the couple had left for London. They hadn't. That evening George escorted them to Liverpool and saw them safely aboard the B & I boat bound for Dublin.

He had previously reserved the required accommodation in the name of Bell. I have often wondered if this choice of pseudonym was chosen, just a little 'tongue in cheek' by George, for it was Ikey Bell who brought the couple together, resulting in possibly the happiest years that Bend Or, who had everything, experienced in his rich and full life.

That evening I spent with Henry Hamilton and his wife. The former was a very shrewd and knowledgeable person when it came to matters concerning agriculture. During the course of the evening I was to learn that he had been at the 'Home Farm' (actually Woodhouse Farm, Aldford – yet another village completely owned by the Duke) since 1920. During that time the Duke had only on three occasions visited the farm, and taken a quick and cursory look at a small number of his world-famous herd.

This filled me with a certain amount of misgiving. I had been used to working for someone who took the keenest interest in his herds and estate. Henry did not lessen my feeling of apprehension by saying he did not think that Dairy Shorthorns of the type we were used to would fit into the scheme of things in Ireland, where beef took precedence over dairying. If this was so I wondered not only at the advisability of the proposed venture, but, also, at the haste at which it was to be implemented. George Ridley, in the course of the afternoon, had stressed that speed was of the essence. The Duke wanted some of his Shorthorns in Ireland!

A week later I crossed to Eire with Ridley and Hamilton. From the boat we took a taxi to the Shelbourne Hotel and checked in. Having been to our rooms we gathered in the entrance hall, before proceeding to the dining room for breakfast. George stopped and looked around, then a smile spread across his face.

"Ah, there they are."

"Who?" I enquired.

"The Duke and Duchess. They crossed on the Mail Boat from Holyhead to Dún Laoghaire last night. Come and meet them."

For a fraction of a second my nerve nearly failed me. It was one thing to hear and talk about a legend, it was another thing to meet one. But there was not time for further thought; George was hurrying across the room, all smiles. The Duke stood up as we reached his table.

He was still strikingly handsome, his greeting warm and most certainly friendly. Like hundreds more before me I was immediately charmed by his manner and personality. He introduced me to the Duchess. I remember well that the first thing that struck me was her eyes and the warmth of her smile. It was easy to see what had attracted 'The Owner' to Miss Sullivan! We stood talking for a few minutes, then the Duke enquired, "When are you coming to Fort William?"

George replied he thought in about three days. We had a number of meetings arranged in Dublin and Maynooth for the remainder of the day and the next one. Then it was his intention to go to Bruree, finally Lismore.

"No, come to lunch tomorrow."

I noticed that the fact a number of appointments, from which he would indirectly derive benefit, would have to be changed, did not enter into his thoughts. For a fraction of a second I saw a flicker of annoyance cross George's face.

"I'll have Hamilton with me, as well as Twist."

"Fine, see you all for lunch tomorrow." He sat down – the audience was over.

Three quarters of an hour later we were in McVeagh's office. High on the agenda was – where was I going to live? A matter that Ridley seemed to think was of minor importance and apparently one to which he had given little thought. One phone call from George McVeagh and the problem was solved. He arranged for us to go and see a large and spacious bed-sitting room in a guesthouse, where they served breakfast and dinner. It was well staffed – one could even put one's shoes out to be cleaned!

It was owned and run by a delightful lady and her daughter. The former was a widow. Less than a year previously she had been the wife of a Master of Hounds, living in a large house on an estate in the centre of Ireland. When the day of reckoning came, following her husband's death, she found that the bank had a far greater interest in the property than she had! Much to my delight George Ridley said the estate would pay. I thought that great! A substantial increase in salary and I hadn't worked for His Grace a month. We returned to McVeagh's office and dealt with a number of urgent matters. Then Ridley turned to McVeagh and asked,

"Can you buy a new car for Michael? The one he owns will never take him around the estates, every week or ten days, for long." Then turning to me. "I think we'd better supply your transport. It wouldn't be fair to ask you to. You'll probably do anything from 25,000 to 30,000 miles a year." He was wrong – it turned out to be nearer 40,000.

Next we went to Maynooth and viewed the dairy farm, Derrinstown. One hundred and sixty-four acres, costing £8,500. My heart sank when I saw it. The house, which was in need of a great deal of renovation, was reached by a rough gravel track and situated about 150 yards from the road. There was a very primitive cow byre, three loose boxes and a very small shed beyond it. It was in fact a mess. George must have noticed the look of disappointment on my face.

"Don't worry, I did tell you that a new set of buildings were required. They will be modelled on the ones on the Eaton Estates."

I wasn't sure I cared for the latter part of the statement. The farm buildings at Eaton, whilst magnificent from many aspects, dated way back into the previous century. George continued. "We have a meeting with the architect and one of Sisk's directors this afternoon."

I studied the plans spread out across the table. Undoubtedly they were all very impressive, even to being built with cut sandstone blocks as at Eaton. At last I looked up. "What's this lot going to cost?"

Sisk's representative cleared his throat and looked slightly confused.

"Well I don't rightly know. Mr Ridley said the work was to be done on a time and materials basis, gave us an idea as to what was wanted, but, above all else stressed that speed was the most important thing. At a rough guess something between £80,000 and £90,000."

I looked at George Ridley.

"Isn't that an awful lot to spend on buildings, even for the Duke, for a property costing eight and a half thousand?" He looked at me for a moment, then laughed.

"You could be right. You're responsible for the Irish estates now, so over to you."

The outcome was a more than adequate set of buildings, plus two modern three-bedroomed bungalows, the house modernized and a roadway put in to the farmyard for £22,500.

The next day we set off early for Lismore, stopping at Cahir to call at the hotel for a cup of coffee and to confirm with Eileen McCool that we would be staying overnight. It was a gorgeous October day. Co. Tipperary was looking its finest as we followed the twisting by-road that led to Clogheen, a remote, but highly colourful village.

A number of the houses and cottages were brightly painted, not just simply whitewashed or with a drab, discoloured cement rendering, as were so many throughout the country. As we climbed up the road from the village to 'The Gap', crossing the Knockmealdown Mountains, I looked back across the vale. The view was spectacular. One which, over the years, I never grew tired of in all its varying moods. Nevertheless, I was very conscious of the fact that, whilst stunningly beautiful on a peerless autumn day, it might be very different in midwinter. A surmise that was to prove frighteningly true on more than one occasion in the future. Often, in winter time, I drove the thirteen miles from Clogheen to Lismore without seeing another vehicle or living soul, frequently through snow, ice and fog.

As we drew near 'The Gap', George pointed out a cairn, about two to three hundred yards from the summit of the mountain on our left. Apparently, years before, a native of Clogheen who had spent most of his adult life in foreign parts, returned to the place of his birth to die. It was his wish that, when the Day of Judgement came, his coffin should be carried to the highest point of the mountain, then stood on end so that he could gaze out across his beloved Co. Tipperary.

Several years later, when I had reason to stop in Clogheen, whilst on the way to Lismore, an aged local sidled up to me and enquired if I had ever seen the cairn. I replied "Yes, frequently." Nothing daunted, he proceeded to give me a detailed account of events leading up to its being. When the poor man died, a magnificent wake was held. The finest fiddlers for miles around attended and dancing, plus a great consumption of porter and not a little poteen, went on until dawn. The time had come, as the narrator so graphically put it, 'to plant the corpse'.

The coffin was loaded onto an ass and cart, amidst much keening from the women who were not going to make the final journey up the mountainside. The cortege of kith and kin set off, that was, so the story went, 'them that were able and not legless'. The party was led by the parish priest, described to me as 'a great man for the hurley* an' a divil for th'hardstuff** so he was'. Black clouds hung over the moun-

* hurley – a traditional Irish game, like hockey and lacrosse
** hardstuff – whiskey

tains, the wind icy. As the party climbed higher the cold increased and the wind became more arctic. At last they reached their destination, just short of 'The Gap'.

Having refreshed themselves with poteen, willing hands grasped the coffin and headed for the summit. All was going well, until snow started blowing about in the wind. The priest exhorted the pallbearers to hurry. As they climbed higher, so the snow increased, until finally His Reverence decided enough was enough and gave the order.

"Up end him boys, 'tis far enough."

Instructions having been quickly completed, prayers were hurriedly said and many hands heaped the stones. My informant grinned, "Wasn't that a grand ending for any man? I'm telling you sorr this talking's terrible thirsty work, so it is." I felt in my pocket and handed him a half-crown. He went off rejoicing, leaving me wondering if there was any truth in the story, or whether the cairn had become 'a cottage industry'.

As we descended into Co. Waterford, the scenery, while still spectacular, had not the grandeur of the Tipperary side. Finally, we approached Lismore, the castle towering over the River Blackwater – a picture of opulent tranquillity. We drove across the bridge and up into the town, although by English standards it was only a good-sized village. We headed out along a road that ran parallel with the river. After a little over a mile we turned in through a gateway and made our way down an avenue lined with trees, towards the river.

Half way along we passed what George told me had been the farm buildings, but which were now being converted into stables. On rounding a bend in the driveway I had my first view of Fort William. A most attractive stone-built house, overlooking the river, with pleasant views and a homely appearance. I immediately understood why, when he found it, George felt a deal just had to be made with Mr Dunne.

As we rounded the final bend, we could see His Grace standing outside the front door. Was he waiting for our arrival, or merely in attendance on the dachshund, Dringalo, who was snuffling around on the drive a few yards from him? Ancient, but much loved by the Duke he was, quite simply, a spoilt little beast with none too sweet a temperament. He was just as likely to have a go at one's ankles, as wag his tail at the pleasure of seeing one. Fortunately, his attacks were of no great moment, for, as I have said, he was ancient and thus nearly toothless!

'The Owner' greeted us warmly and ushered us into the house. The hall was spacious and comfortably furnished but, in my opinion as, indeed, it was in the opinion of many others, spoilt by the massive chandelier that seemed to dominate the décor. After a few remarks about the wonderful weather for October, the Duke led us through to the dining room and, waving towards a sideboard laden with bottles, bade us help ourselves to whatever we fancied. Having charged our glasses we went through to the library to join the Duchess.

She was, as at our first meeting, charming. She told me that Captain Fitzgerald was coming to lunch and that afterwards there were several matters she wished to discuss with us. A few minutes later Fitz was shown in by John Lynch, the young resident butler at the Fort. Introductions and formalities over, Fitz was told to go and get himself a drink. He had a distinct twang when he spoke, the product of many years spent in Canada and the United States. I was to learn that he also had a peculiar habit, when agitated, of making a movement with his left arm as though he was cracking a whip. At the same time he prefaced any remark he was about to make on the subject that had disturbed him with 'Aa-ah gee'.

Lunch was pleasant and we discussed many subjects, but little that related to the Irish properties, except just as we'd finished and were about to leave the table. The Duke suddenly turned to me and enquired,

"Tell me, Twist, when are you planning to bring over the first consignment of Shorthorns?"

"As soon as the new farm buildings are completed and we can reserve the Quarantine State at Glasgow."

"Oh! Oh! Nothing wrong with my cattle is there Hamilton?"

"Nothing Your Grace."

"Well then, what's all this quarantine nonsense?"

I explained that it was an Irish Government regulation that all cloven-hoofed animals entering the country had to first be quarantined for three weeks, so as to avoid any risk of Foot and Mouth Disease. This was greeted with a ducal snort as 'The Owner' headed for the door.

"Come on Ridley, I've a number of things I want to talk to you about. And Twist, I want my cattle over here by the spring." With that he walked out of the room. The Duchess rose and smiled sweetly at Henry.

"Perhaps you might like to walk up to the farm and meet Lawlor, the steward. I told him to watch out for you. We'll have tea at four o'clock." Then, turning to Fitz and me, she continued, "Come on, I'll get a coat, then we'll go down the garden and I'll show you what I want doing." About an hour and a half later, having discussed a number of possible projects, Fitz enquired,

"Is that the lot, Duchess?"

"Not quite. There's a little job I want attending to in the house." Fitz looked puzzled as we made our way back up the path. Sisks had only just finished work on the inside and whilst there were a few minor exterior jobs to complete, they had moved out to work on the stables whilst the Duke and Duchess were in residence. Nancy led the way up the stairs and along the corridor, finally turning into a bathroom – her bathroom. It was situated between her and the Duke's bedrooms. There was a door leading from it into Bend Or's room. Indicating the door, the Duchess said,

"I want that bricked up. He will keep wandering in while I'm having a bath."

Then, sounding almost as though it was an afterthought,

added, "He will leave it open and it causes a draft." With that she was gone. Fitz's expression was a study, then the left arm jerked up and cracked down.

"Aa-ah gee, I guess that's the only bit of excitement the poor old bugger has." I made no comment, mine not to reason why, but in the years that followed, when television had invaded our homes, and Larry Grayson became a popular comedian with his catch phrase – 'shut that door' – my mind would go back to that October afternoon in 1947!

That evening, back at the hotel, I talked at length to George about the Irish estates. At last I knew what I was talking about and it was very obvious that life was likely to become hectic in the not-too-distant future.

I asked George, "Was the Duke serious about having some Shorthorns at Maynooth by the spring?"

"Absolutely, you'd better believe it too. It's all yours now – one less thing for me to worry about."

We had excellent steaks for dinner, followed by some quite passable Irish cheese. Whilst Henry and George were chatting with various members of the McCool family, I decided to take a walk around the square outside the hotel. As I left, I saw there was a small crowd gathered round a truck on the far side. On it was a man who was haranguing those about him. I heard the word 'Westminster', hurried across and stood quietly in the background.

The speaker was ranting on about Ireland for the Irish. The country didn't want any Sassenachs, like the Duke of Westminster, or any other 'bloody Englishman' owning properties in Eire; even if they brought in money and gave employment. They should be thrown out. It had been done before, it could be done again! I returned thoughtfully to the hotel. Was I mad coming to live in a country where, apparently, we weren't welcome? I enquired of Pat John, Eileen McCool's eldest brother, who the firebrand was across the square.

"Oh him. That's Sean McBride. You don't want to pay

any attention to him. He's a fanatic, leader of Clan na Poblachta, the republican party. Ireland for the Irish and all that sort of thing. He conveniently forgets about the thousands and thousands of Irish who make their living in Britain and whom this country could not possibly support." Then with a laugh, "Thanks to the Pope, labour's our biggest export." In the twenty-three wonderful years I lived in Eire, that night in Cahir was the only time I heard an outburst against the British.

The next morning we motored across to Bruree and I met Stephen and Ursula Vernon for the first time. He, poor man, had contracted poliomyelitis in North Africa during the war and could only walk with difficulty. Although officially stud manager, he seldom appeared in the yard until late morning and was very dependent on Tom Beedleston, the excellent stud groom.

I sensed a certain amount of animosity towards me from him, when George introduced us and explained that, in the future, I would be looking after the Duke's interests in Ireland. Ursula, on the other hand, was charming and we hit it off immediately. She, like the Duke, had a great love for dachshunds – she had two. A few years later this love and obsession led to high drama, when one of her dachsies died.

The first I knew about it was when I received a phone call from a somewhat distraught Tom Beedleston, asking what he should do. The whole place was in an uproar. He had been sent for by the Major at, for him, an early hour. With difficulty, through choking sobs, he had told Beedleston that one of Lady Ursula's dachshunds was dead. He was to have a grave dug in front of the house, which was then to be lined with flowers from the hothouse. It was midwinter. When this was done, he was to go and see the Protestant rector for the parish and ask him to come and conduct a service.

All had gone according to plan until Tom had gone to see the cleric. The latter had been most incensed at the suggestion and his answer had been a most emphatic 'no'. It seemed that Lady Ursula was seething. She had instructed Beedleston to phone me immediately to ask me to contact the Archbishop and persuade him to intercede on her behalf. After telling Tom to leave it with me, I put a call through to Bruree House. It was some minutes before a sobbing Ursula came to the phone. Having been suitably sympathetic, I asked, "Are you sure he was of our calling?"

"Of course, I'm a Protestant."

"Ah, but you're not really certain. Why not ask Father McCarthy to come and say a few words?" The latter was a delightful fox-hunting priest, who lived in a nearby parish and was everlastingly begging a mount off Lady Ursula. His rather aged and inferior horse seemed to be almost permanently lame! Ursie thought it was a great idea. She would telephone the good Father immediately and, please, would I come down and spend the night – she and Stephen were feeling so miserable. As I had intended going to Bruree the next day anyway, I readily agreed.

When Lady Ursula had phoned the sporting priest, he had replied, "An' why not? Aren't we all God's creatures. How does tomorrow morning suit you? That yoke of mine is hopping lame an' I have nothing to ride tomorrow, an' it is one of the best meets of the season."

The answer had been a firm 'no'. It had to be right away, the grave was ready. The funeral could not be put off. When I reached Bruree, just in time to change for dinner, I was greeted most affectionately by Ursie. She kissed me on both cheeks and then pressed a large gin and tonic into my hand. She gazed at me with those soft limpid eyes, now slightly watery, which I had come to know so well – I knew her troubles of the morning were now behind her!

I found Father McCarthy comfortably ensconced in front of a roaring log fire, a glass of whiskey in his hand, and a smile on his face. He had a mount for the meet of the hounds next day!

3
Ridley Becomes Supremo

On my return to Chester things took on a different complexion. No longer was I sitting around 'twiddling my thumbs', looking for something to do. I had plenty to keep me occupied. I redesigned the farm buildings for Derrinstown. Sent off my ideas to the architect in Dublin. Wrote to Sisks, stressing that work must be commenced early in November, that is if we were to get anywhere near meeting the Duke's deadline. I asked George Ridley if 'The Owner' would wish to see the plans. His snort was derisive as he assured me that His Grace was not interested in such things. Much time was spent with Henry Hamilton, making a provisional selection of cows and heifers to be included in the first shipment to Ireland.

I spent all the time I could with Bill Bryan. I wanted to learn about the House of Grosvenor and acquire as much useful information as possible. Sadly, Bend Or had no direct heir. He'd had a son, Edward George Hugh, Earl of Grosvenor, but alas he lived to be barely five years of age. He had died following an operation for appendicitis.

The Duke was devastated by his son's death, which heightened the rift that already existed between him and the first duchess, formerly Constance Cornwallis West. Basil Kerr told me that, from the moment of the little boy's death, the marriage was virtually over.

The situation was not helped by Bend Or's infatuation with the actress Gertie Millar. Ikey Bell always said that, if he'd had the courage, the Duke would have married her. As it was she was his mistress for a number of years. Ikey always maintained that Bend Or visited her for a couple of hours on his wedding night, such was his burning desire for this daughter of a Bradford mill worker. Whilst Gertie failed in her attempt to catch a Duke, she did the next best thing and married an Earl, for she became the Countess of Dudley!

One day I asked Bill Bryan the origin of the name Bend Or. I knew, of course, that it was the name of one of the first Duke's four Derby winners. But what did it mean? Bill told me its origin dated back to the fourteenth century. King Richard II was at war with Scotland, amongst his knights was Sir Robert Grosvenor. Prior to entering into battle his archers mustered around his banner, 'Azure, a bend or'.

Apparently, one Sir Richard Scrope, Baron Bolton, claimed that the escutcheon being displayed by Sir Robert was that of the Scrope family. A bitter row ensued which grew to such magnitude that the dispute was brought before the Court of Chivalry for settlement in the autumn of 1385. It was not until the following spring that the Duke of Gloucester, representing the King, gave judgement in favour of Sir Richard. Sir Robert was offered arms 'Azure, a bend or' with a plain bordure, Argent for difference.' He refused. The matter dragged on until the spring of 1390, when finally the King intervened. The arms, from that day onwards, for the Grosvenors were to be 'Azure a garb or' – a gold wheat sheaf on a blue background. The findings of the Court of Chivalry, together with King Richard's ruling, are recorded on a parchment which at the time was kept at Eaton Hall. Centuries later the first Duke, recalling the dispute, took the name Bend Or for his magnificent chestnut colt. Subsequently, when the latter had won a place of great esteem and affection with the Duke, he dubbed his grandson, then the Viscount Belgrave, Bend Or.

About ten days after our return from Ireland, Ridley told me he had to go to London and wished me to accompany him. We were driven over to Crewe, from where we caught the London train. We had a first-class compartment to ourselves for the entire journey.

This provided a wonderful opportunity to talk, free of

interruptions. George, for the first time, told me of his concern regarding the future of the Grosvenor millions, and the lack of either initiative or concern by both staff and advisers to take any positive action to minimize what would be crippling death duties when the Duke died.

George had already had several talks with his employer on this subject. They had not been easy to begin with, due to the Duke taking the attitude that he had no intention of dying for many years to come! George had persevered, even at the risk of causing offence and putting his job in jeopardy. Persuasion won and His Grace agreed that it would be the height of folly to let the Labour Government, or indeed any other government, get their hands on the family fortune.

Having agreed that action should be taken, it was certainly something that 'The Owner' considered did not require his full and undivided attention. The bulk of the capital was held in trust, but was of such magnitude that, despite paying Income Tax at the rate of nineteen shillings and sixpence in the pound, the Duke derived all the income he could possible require, without concerning himself with the management of the principal. The vast majority of the Grosvenor wealth was invested in such a way as to attract the maximum death duties – eighty per cent!

In the past some steps had been taken, but these faded into insignificance when compared with what Ridley had in mind. For example, in 1933 the Duke and his advisers had obtained an act through Parliament, which would have allowed him to make over £350,000 each from the Trust to his two daughters, Lady Ursula and Lady Mary. Having obtained this somewhat unique concession, nothing more was done and the matter was held in abeyance. Whether this was due to lassitude on the part of those administering the Duke's affairs, or the latter's disinclination to release such a vast sum to his two daughters, I never discovered. I would suspect the latter.

Whilst £350,000 does not sound a staggeringly large sum

these days, at the time it was untold wealth. A loaf of bread could be bought for two pence and a gallon of petrol for less than a shilling – 5p in present day currency! Whatever the reason, a unique opportunity was missed. When George Ridley eventually learned of the act of Parliament, he implemented its concession as quickly as possible, but alas too late. The Duke died before the required five years had elapsed that would make the gifts free of death duties. Through such neglect family fortunes could be lost!

George told me, almost excitedly, of his plans. These were to transfer money from stocks and shares into agricultural properties. Not just any old ones. They had to be gilt-edged ones, where he could be sure of not only regaining the principal invested, but also of showing reasonable capital appreciation. Any monies so invested would immediately provide a thirty-six per cent saving in tax when 'The Owner' died.

In conjunction with this saving George visualized a vast forestry investment. All planting and future maintenance would be done under Schedule D. All chargeable against Income Tax, recoverable at nineteen shillings and sixpence in the pound, thus establishing a veritable goldmine for future Grosvenors. It seemed that the possibilities in this sphere were endless. Woodlands, that is mature ones, assessed under Schedule B were to be purchased and felled. When this happened monies obtained would be free of tax and would be money in the Duke's hand. The felled area could then be reassessed under Schedule D and a further forest developed virtually at the expense of the Treasury! George paused in outlining his master plan and looked at me.

"You know, Michael, it's criminal. All the years that have been wasted and not a bloody thing has been done worth mentioning to safeguard the future! I may as well be honest with you, it's not just the Grosvenors I'm thinking of – it's all of us, our jobs, our homes, our futures. I'll do everything in my power for the well-being of 'The Owner', but at the end of the day I want to feel that I'll be secure – no worries when

I reach retirement. I want that for you and many others who will have to give everything in order to reach our objective, in the now limited time available."

I was impressed. They were words that came vividly to my mind some seven years later!

Ridley continued to expound. He told me that the Duke's Will was totally out of date, but, so far, no one had persuaded him to revise it. A matter high on George's list of priorities. It was at this juncture that I was to learn that the heir to the title was not automatically heir to the Grosvenor millions. There was no entailment of wealth. The next in line for the dukedom was one of Bend Or's many cousins – Captain Robert Grosvenor.

The first Duke had certainly been prolific, having fathered fifteen children from his two marriages, but not particularly noteworthy in Victorian days when large families were the norm. As it turned out, Robert did not inherit the title, he died only a short time before the Duke.

The 3rd Duke, William, was another cousin. He received none of the wealth that was associated with the title. Bend Or, many years before he died, had made ample provision so that William could live in comfort, if not splendour.

It would not be an exaggeration to say that William was something of an eccentric. I never met him, but knew his sister, Dorothy, very well. She had married Richard Mack, Captain of the Duke's yacht. She and her husband Dick (incidentally her third husband), my wife and I, dined together frequently, to be followed by long sessions playing Canasta – then all the rage. It was Dorothy who told me that her brother was a bit unstable.

She had us in fits of laughter one evening, telling us how her brother kept some breed of poultry – I think they were Light Sussex. When no one was around he would let them out into the garden and then secrete himself behind a bush, armed with a sword. Any hens foolish enough to come within his orbit he charged, brandishing his sword and, should some luckless fowl not be fleet enough of foot, it would be in grave danger of losing its head. Dot told us that, after one or two such forays, those close to William persuaded him to give up keeping hens and, instead, turn his attention to ducks, which could live unmolested on their pond!

According to his sister, the third Duke was not a happy man. He may well have been a little eccentric, but not to a degree that made him unaware of what he had missed out on. Nor was Dorothy a happy lady when the 2nd Duke died, for she too had been hoping for 'a slice of the cake'. However, she did get a title as sister to a Duke and became Lady Mack. The Sunday Express so aptly headed a piece about her 'Once More a Lady'. A title was nothing new to her, in view of her somewhat chequered matrimonial past!

She had a most vitriolic tongue and, like Ursula Vernon, no love for George Ridley. She always referred to George as 'the bloody little road-sweeper'. Apparently, her first memory of him was in his early days in the Forestry Department at Eaton, when he and others were sweeping the Saighton drive on the estate! It really hurt when she wanted a loan from her cousin and Bend Or had told her to talk to Ridley. Eventually I dealt with the matter. I met her at the Royal Dublin Horse Show. I had never spoken to her before.

My brief was clear. 'The Owner' really did not mind whether he lent his cousin the money she required or not. If he did, it was to be entirely on the terms stipulated by him. (For 'him' read Ridley.) We met under the clock in the middle of the showground. After ten minutes I persuaded her to come round to accepting the terms that the Duke required for the loan. She agreed. Then she looked me straight in the eye and said,

"I suppose you think you're bloody clever."

"No, but I think you could be a bloody difficult woman."

A smile spread across her face and then she burst out laughing.

"Come on, come and have a drink. You and I talk the same language." We went up the stairs to the bar. I was surprised to find that she was virtually a teetotaller – it didn't fit in with the tough man-eating reputation that she had! That drink was the start of a friendship that lasted many years.

George continued to fill me in with regard to his future plans. He envisaged a rapid switch of money from stocks and shares into land. This he assured me had to be done as quickly as possible, which really meant as quickly as he could persuade the Duke that the matter was urgent and should not be delayed.

At the time of our conversation the agricultural estates were Eaton, Lochmore in Sutherlandshire, the Halkyn Estate in North Wales and Mimizan in France; although the latter hardly qualified for inclusion in the overall scheme to avoid death duties. How Ridley was going to achieve his ambitions was not quite clear, for, he told me, he was receiving a very considerable amount of opposition to his plans from those who administered the London Estates, namely a firm of solicitors and the Duke's accountants. It was unlikely that they would relinquish control of such an obviously lucrative and desirable tenure without considerable, if concealed, resistance.

George admitted to being somewhat in awe of those concerned who, it appeared, were inclined to treat him as 'a country bumpkin'. However, he assured me, once he had completely sold his ideas to the Duke, then they could watch out, for nothing was going to stand in his way. For a fraction of a second, I saw that hard look I had glimpsed the first day we had met.

George had a great ally in Gordon Saunders, senior partner of John D Woods of Berkeley Square, estate agents who specialized in large agricultural properties and who had already supplied details of several which might prove to be suitable investments. One thing seemed patently obvious: no one man could cope unaided with what George planned. I put this point to him.

"Agreed, I'm already negotiating with John Saunders, Gordon's son, to join us as my assistant. You and he will be my lieutenants as far as the agricultural properties are concerned. We'll need an agent on each estate and the best forester in the country." He laughed. "That's if I can persuade the Duke to play ball. It's tricky, he's not very keen on discussing what will happen after his demise!"

The following Sunday I lunched with George and his charming wife, Mary. The former was in a very ebullient mood. He'd talked to the Duke, when in London, probably more frankly than His Grace had ever been spoken to before. George had really laid it on the line. To his surprise Bend Or had been remarkably receptive to his ideas and fully endorsed his agent's views. He agreed that it would be positively criminal to allow the current government, or indeed any other, to get their hands on the Grosvenor capital, accumulated over many centuries, for they were, after all, already taking nineteen shillings and six pence in Income Tax out of every pound his investments earned! There seemed to be only one snag; the Duke did not want to be bothered having to sign papers implementing agreed plans. This he overcame on 14 December 1947 – he gave George written authority to act on his behalf in connection with all his estates and affairs in general. Quite possibly the shrewdest move any Grosvenor had ever made since Bend Or's forebears reputedly arrived in this country with William the Conqueror! George Kershaw Ridley had become Chief Agent. To all intents and purposes he controlled the Grosvenor millions!

4
Land Agent Turned Smuggler

It was a cold, misty morning early in November 1947 as the 'Munster' edged alongside the North Wall, Dublin. Dick Powley stood beside me as we watched the final docking manoeuvres from the deck. He'd only remained at Roundhill for a month after I had left, before returning to the Eaton Estate to stay with his mother. Henry Hamilton had been quick to take him on as head herdsman, to go to Ireland when required.

I had slept little during the crossing. Not that my bunk hadn't been comfortable – it had – and the sea had been like the proverbial millpond, it was just excitement and thinking about the future that had kept me awake, my mind racing. My thoughts were interrupted by a steward, already liberally tipped, who, accompanied by two porters, had come to collect our luggage. In a matter of minutes it was lined up on the trestle tables in the warehouse that doubled as a customs hall.

To my surprise I was greeted by the senior officer on duty. He told me he'd been advised of my pending arrival by George McVeagh. I had my shotguns with me and, although the licenses were in order, George wanted to be sure there would be no problems. Having cleared customs, Dick and I went our separate ways, he to meet Pat John McCool and take delivery of a new ten hundredweight Ford van; while I took a taxi to No. 4 Dartmouth Road, which was to be my home for the next two years.

Having settled in, I breakfasted before setting off to keep an appointment with McVeagh. We had much to discuss. I still didn't know if I had any transport and was anxious to learn what he'd been able to do regarding this. Cars were really at a premium, both new and second hand and I was relieved to hear he'd been successful. He'd obtained, I know not how, a new Standard 9. Not exactly what I would have chosen for the distances I would be driving, but, as George rightly said, a small new car was a better proposition than a large pre-war one with an indeterminable mileage and an unknown history.

When we had finished our immediate business, we walked up Kildare Street to the Shelbourne Garage, where I took possession of my transport taxed, insured and ready for the road. There was even a road map provided and a street map of Dublin. Having introduced me to the owner of the garage George departed, leaving me to write a cheque – the first on one of the Duke's accounts. Formalities over, I was handed a book of petrol coupons – five gallons for a month. Not a lot of use in view of the mileage I anticipated doing. However, I wasn't unduly concerned and asked the way to the office dealing with petrol rationing. I had no doubt that, as in England, supplementary petrol would be available for agricultural purposes.

I found the office with ease and was greeted by a remarkably pretty and vivacious girl. I explained my needs. She gave me a charming smile and said,

"Well, 'tis easy to see you're not a priest, so you must be a doctor."

I matched smile with smile and explained who I was. That my employer was already employing a large number of people, directly and indirectly, and that this figure would be greatly increased in the near future. The reply remained the same.

"Sorry! Only priests and doctors get the supplementary."

I tried persuasion. I cajoled. I even tried 'if I cannot get petrol to run the Duke's affairs he'll probably pull out of Ireland altogether.' The answer remained the same – 'No'. Then this charming, but obstinate, colleen took a look right and left, to make sure no-one was within hearing distance, and crooked a finger at me, leaning forward across the desk in a conspiratorial manner.

"'Tis easy to tell you're a stranger. You can buy all the coupons you want from the turf-men in the park." I obviously looked confused, so she enlightened me. The turf-men were the lorry drivers carting what to me, a Sassenach, was peat.

The park was Phoenix Park, that vast area on the outskirts of the city where the Viceregal Lodge, now the President's residence, stands in all its grandeur. I thanked my informant and followed the River Liffey out to the entrance to the park. Quickly I was driving parallel to what seemed a never-ending clamp of turf. After about a mile I came upon several lorries. These were piled high with the fuel that had so largely replaced imported coal through the war years. One lorry was being unloaded, its contents meticulously stacked. Several of the waiting drivers stood around, smoking, chatting and enjoying the late autumn sunshine. I stopped and got out of the car. Immediately I was greeted with friendly smiles and cheerful 'good mornings'. I passed a few remarks about the weather and then said,

"I'm told I can buy petrol coupons here?"

There was complete silence. Then a giant of a man strode over to me. "D'yer not know 'tis illegal to sell the coupons?"

I almost panicked and ran. Of course it was, but I hadn't really considered it. After all, I had received my information from an official source, so to speak! I explained that I was new to the country and I had been advised by a charming young lady at the office to drive out and ask about buying coupons. A smile spread across the giant's face.

"Begob, that'll have been me niece, so it will. A grand wee girl an' a terrible help to us poor workin' men. How many would you like sorr? Them's half-a-crown per gallon."

That was a lot dearer than the actual petrol, but so what! After all, I did work for the richest man in the British Isles. He certainly would not be pleased if I could not get around his estates and do my job. I took forty, much to the delight of the vendors and with promises of all I wanted in the future, I headed back into Dublin. It was in fact the only time I had to buy any. There seemed to be no shortage of petrol, none of the garages with whom we dealt, from the various estates, were interested in coupons.

That afternoon I had a long session at Derrinstown with the architect and Michael O'Driscoll, one of Sisk's directors. When I said that work would have to be completed by the end of March, both my companions laughed. Quite impossible. I explained that His Grace wanted the first consignment of Shorthorns on the farm by the Spring. Michael O'Driscoll laughed again.

"I'm afraid 'want' will be his master. Tell His Grace that we have a saying in this country – 'When the good God made time, he made plenty of it'. He'll just have to be patient." It was a message I did not pass on to the Duke – I didn't think he would be impressed!

That evening when I returned to Dartmouth Road there was a message for me to phone Ridley immediately. This I did. George sounded upset. Apparently, the Duke had got to know that the Vernons, in the few months they had been at Bruree, had run up a bill with one Davey O'Donnell of Croome in excess of £4,000, all for drink. Quite a phenomenal amount particularly when compared with the cost of the stud farm, with its house, magnificent buildings, land and cottages. But this wasn't the worry – it had been done in the Duke's name! He was, George said, extremely displeased.

George went on to say that he had telephoned Stephen Vernon, and the latter had claimed it was a perfectly legitimate charge against the stud – entertaining! The upshot was that I was to leave first thing next morning for Bruree and sort the matter out. I did not relish the idea, but it was an order, so there was no arguing. I asked what I was to do if the Vernons would not accept responsibility. The reply was, "The Duke says you are to settle the matter. Fortunately he has not said how. If the worst comes to the worst you will have to pay.

We can sort it out later with the Vernons. Whatever happens we cannot have it rumoured around Ireland that the Duke does not pay his bills."

The session I had with Stephen and Ursula, the next day, was not a happy one. The former was openly hostile, indeed rude, whilst Ursula spent the entire time I was there decrying her father. After nearly two hours of fruitless discussion the butler entered, lunch was served. I was not invited. I was furious. I had achieved nothing and the nearest place I could get something to eat was Limerick – nineteen miles away! To get there I had to go through Croome. I stopped to see Davey O'Donnell – known as 'the Mayor'.

'The Mayor' was an engaging personality and, like many establishments in the country in Ireland, dealt in virtually everything. He greeted me warmly and insisted on taking me off immediately to his stable yard at the back of the shop. Here he tried hard to sell me a horse for a quite exorbitant price. Having failed in this, we retired to the parlour where, without consulting me, he poured two enormous whiskeys. At last we got down to business. I explained that such a sum for drink could in no way be justified as a charge against the Duke's stud farm and that the responsibility had to be that of the Vernons. He nodded sagely, fully agreed, and excused himself, saying he'd be back in a few minutes. It was a quarter of an hour before he returned. Smiling broadly, he handed me a sheet of paper. It was an account for fertilizer, building materials, even the gelding I had been looking at was included. The various items added up to exactly the same amount as the bill for the drink! Before commenting I enquired how I was going to explain the absence of the gelding when we came to do the annual valuation and stocktaking.

"Ah sure, couldn't you be saying he'd broken a leg and had to be shot?"

Bearing in mind what George Ridley had said to me about all tax evasion having to be one hundred percent within the law, I declined Davey's solution to the problem.

He was quite unruffled.

"Was just a suggestion, so it was, but I must be having me money. 'Tis a terrible amount for a man like me to be owed an' hasn't His Grace a side more money than me?"

Grudgingly, I paid the original invoice. Subsequently the bookkeeper put it through the stud account as entertainment. At the end of the year, much to my surprise, the auditors didn't even query it! That evening I phoned Ridley and told him of Davey's alternative account. He fully supported what I had done. He again emphasized that, whilst tax evasion was the name of the game, everything towards this end had to be legitimate and completely within the law. A ruling which, as far as I am aware, was always most scrupulously adhered to.

Men seemed to swarm like ants over the building site at Derrinstown. Michael O'Driscoll had taken me seriously about the work having to be finished by the end of March, although he said it was really asking the impossible. In actual fact I had given myself a month's grace, or at least I thought I had. There would be no point in having cattle on the land until there was an abundance of grass and that would not be until the end of April or early May.

With this in mind Henry Hamilton was to make application for the Ministry of Agriculture's Quarantine Station at Glasgow for the last two weeks in April and the first week in May. Imagine my horror when he telephoned to say that the Ministry had said the whole station would only be available on 24 February, or late in September. Common sense decreed it had to be the latter. The former would mean that the shipment would arrive in Ireland on 16 March. The buildings could not possibly be ready in time and certainly there would be no grass. I made my views known to George Ridley and told him that I had written to the Duke explaining the situation.

George was not encouraging. He said he didn't think 'The Owner' would be very receptive to my suggestion that it would be prudent to wait until September. He was right. I received a telegram which read something as follows:

> "Will call to see my Shorthorns at Derrinstown in the Spring. Westminster."

The next day, for the first time in my life, I travelled by air. I flew from Dublin to London in an Aer Lingus DC3, a two-and-three-quarter hour flight to Northolt. I went straight to the Ministry of Agriculture and pleaded that we might have the Quarantine Station approximately two months later, but to no avail. The gentleman I saw was most pleasant, but firm. The answer was 'No'. He, quite reasonably, explained that there were other people to be considered as well as the Duke of Westminster. Further, that if we didn't confirm almost at once we'd lose the February date. Desperate, I confirmed.

I had dinner that night with George Ridley. He said the Duke would be delighted to hear the news and that he, George, had great faith in me and gaily assured me that I'd manage.

As we were parting he enquired, "Are you coming over to your home for Christmas?" I replied that had been my intention, but that it now looked as though I might be laying concrete blocks at Derrinstown!

He ignored my sarcasm and said, "Good. I've a list of things I'd like you to bring over for me and, by the way, 'The Owner' would like you to bring him half a dozen bottles of Scotch – you know how impossible it is to get over here, even for someone like him. You could bring a few bottles for me as well."

There was certainly more Scotch whisky available in Ireland than in England, but once imported, one wasn't allowed to take it out again. Travellers had to go through customs both on leaving and entering the country. George's final words that evening as we parted were, "Don't forget the Scotch. The Duke will be very disappointed if he doesn't get it. I'd come over via Holyhead if I was you and use the Duke's labels. I'll have some sent to you."

It wasn't until a few days later, when talking to Bill Bryan on the telephone that I understood the significance of George's suggestion that I go to England via Holyhead. Apparently, all the customs officers, the stationmaster, in fact anyone in authority there, received a large turkey at Christmas and, many of them, a salmon from the estate in Scotland during the summer. One of the reasons for Bill phoning me was to say that 'The Owner' wanted me to discover how many customs officers there were at Dún Laoghaire, get their home addresses and make sure that each received a nice plump turkey at Christmas, with best wishes from His Grace. As Bill explained, there was no question of it being a bribe, for the Duke could and would quite happily pay any duty that goods in his possession might incur – it was just a sign of his thoughtful and generous nature.

Bill went on to say that it was very advantageous for us lesser mortals to use the Duke's labels – lightly crossing out the large 'W' and equally lightly writing in our own name on the distinctive red label.

Whisky was a problem. It was comparatively easy to obtain one bottle, but a case, that was another matter. I had planned to take a couple of bottles over for my father, but with the Duke wanting six and George three, it was going to be difficult to get enough, never mind transport!

A few nights later I was staying at Cahir House Hotel. I'd had dinner and was sitting talking to Pat John McCool and his sister, having just ordered a new tractor for Fort William. I casually brought the topic of conversation round to Scotch whisky. Eileen declared there would be no problem in acquiring a case, the problem would be getting it out of the country. The customs, she assured me, were always on the lookout for such contraband, particularly around Christmas time. As we talked a tall, good looking, young priest walked into the bar.

Eileen greeted him warmly, then, turning to me said, "Here's your answer. Father Pat will take it for you."

"Take what?"

My need was quickly explained. The good priest smiled.

"No problem, but one condition, Michael. When you collect it from the presbytery we crack a bottle."

Greatly relieved, I willingly agreed.

On 21 December I left Dún Laoghaire on the day boat. I had three large suitcases. Rationing was still very much in force in Great Britain, the amount of meat allowed being miniscule. I had 20 lbs of steak with me, also Irish whiskey and gin. The latter was produced in Ireland, so there was no problem taking it out of the country. The trouble might come at Holyhead, but there would be no question of confiscation, just a matter of paying duty. When I arrived by taxi at the pier there were about a dozen people standing dejectedly around. The ferry had been three hours late getting in, due to terrible weather, and, as yet, no one was being allowed on board. I dumped my cases on the pavement and turned to pay the driver. As I did so a porter detached himself from a number that stood by the entrance and walked over to my cases. Having examined the labels, he looked up and smiled.

"I'm Tommy, I always look after His Grace. Don't think we've had you with us before Major Twist." I was everlastingly being called 'Major' in Ireland – I'd almost come to believe I was one!

"Come on sir, I'll take you through to customs." The latter chatted happily as they chalked my cases and told me to thank His Grace for the turkeys – they were magnificent. Meanwhile Tommy had disappeared. He returned within a few minutes with the chief steward. I received full ducal treatment, being ushered aboard immediately. The *hoi polloi* were another hour before they were allowed through to customs! The steward asked if I had a cabin booked. I said that I hadn't. I didn't think I would require one on a day crossing. This, however, appeared to be considered negative thinking. The crossing to Ireland had been one of the worst my friend had experienced in fourteen years. It was unlikely to be much better for the return trip. I would be well advised to have somewhere to lay my head.

Although a good sailor, I gave way to persuasion and was immediately ushered not to a cabin, but a stateroom! I raised an eyebrow, but what the hell! I had a meeting in London next day, so travelling was chargeable to expenses. I tipped the chief steward, apparently to his satisfaction, for he immediately told me that when we reached our destination I was to remain in my cabin. He would come and collect me and organise a porter. It was a rough crossing, very rough. I spent quite a while on the lee side of the deck, enjoying the wildness of the sea. Around midday I made my way to the restaurant for a meal. There was no one in it. Not that there were more than a handful of passengers; the traffic was all back to Ireland for the festive season.

I stood on the deck as we made our way into port. When the ship was made fast I returned and stood outside my cabin. I watched as a gangplank was brought into position towards the stern. The fifteen to twenty passengers were already queuing, waiting to disembark. I began to feel uneasy, had the chief steward forgotten me? It was then I noticed a second gangplank had already been fixed in position towards the bow. Within minutes, via this exclusive route, I was escorted ashore and ushered through to customs.

My friend, the steward, politely introduced me to a senior customs officer as His Grace's agent from Ireland, then asked if I had a seat reserved on the London train. I hadn't. Smiling, he told me to remain where I was when I'd finished with customs – a mere formality. Minutes later he was back, accompanied by the assistant stationmaster. It seemed that he too was on the turkey list! He had with him a porter who took charge of my cases. I was escorted to a first-class compartment – blazoned across the door was a notice which read 'Reserved'. Such was the power of the red label!

The following morning I had a long session with George Ridley and met Derek Turner, who was shortly to take over the management of the Duke's London office. Having had a most enjoyable and interesting lunch with them, I made my way to the presbytery. After ringing the bell several times an aged priest appeared and eyed me through a grille in the door. I asked for Father Pat. I was told he was rather busy. Would anyone else do? The answer was definitely 'no'. I must see Father Pat. Grudgingly and audibly grumbling, the ancient cleric ushered me into a small and dingy room.

I must have waited at least fifteen minutes before Father Pat entered, bearing the case of whiskey. After a most cheerful greeting he rummaged in the nether regions of his cassock and produced two glasses. I opened a bottle and we settled down for a good chat about 'the old country'. I learned that my companion was a keen hunting man. His ambition as a boy had been to be a jump jockey, but, alas, weight outstripped ambition and so his hopes in that direction were gone. Instead he fulfilled his mother's greatest desire and entered the church. When I eventually left it was with eleven bottles. As Father Pat put it, "we'd done a power of good to the twelfth".

I was interested to note I received no word of thanks from 'The Owner'. Perhaps smuggling was considered part of my job. Time appeared to endorse this assumption. It seemed that smuggling was considered rather 'the thing' to do – a jolly jape for one and all! The Duchess ordered a roll-on corset in Dublin, for which she was not asked for clothing coupons. It seemed she was disinclined to bring it out of the country herself. She asked Bill Bryan to do so. Being of slimmish build, Bill decided to don the garment before venturing through customs on each occasion. It was, he said, very tight and he received some very odd looks as he positively minced his way gaily through customs!

The Christmas after the whisky incident I was again pressed into service. Two sets of the Duke's racing colours had been made by Tysons in Dublin. Being his registered colours they were, of course, no use to anyone else. Stephen

Vernon, I think it was, volunteered to take them to England, but they were taken off him when leaving the North Wall, Dublin. The Duke was not pleased. In due course, like most contraband, they were put up for sale by auction. One of George McVeagh's staff attended and bought them at one shilling per set. Shortly after, the Duke came to Ireland and McVeagh told 'The Owner' that the silks had been recovered. When I saw the Duke a day or two later, he told me I was to bring them over to England the next time I came. Further, he said he didn't want them taken by customs again, he wanted them at Eaton.

I must say I felt slightly aggrieved. There was he about to return to England via Holyhead, the chances of his luggage being opened were negligible, and he would be accompanied by at least three servants, but he had no intention of doing any 'smuggling' himself. If anyone got into trouble it was not going to be him!

When the time came I took a leaf out of Bill Bryan's book and decided to wear the wretched things. I could just get them on, but no way could I button them. The covers for the jockeys' headgear, with their stiff peaks, posed something of a problem. Eventually I pushed them down inside the back of my pants, one either side. What I hadn't allowed for was how warm two layers of silks would be! When I left Dartmouth Road I had donned a heavy overcoat, it was a cold night. By the time I reached my cabin the sweat was pouring off me! The following morning in Liverpool it was bitter, but there was I walking around with my overcoat hung over my arm. A young and eager customs officer felt sure there was something hidden in it and took it off me. He spent at least five minutes examining it! Again, there was no question of a thank you from 'The Owner', confirming in my mind that being agent to The Most Noble Hugh Richard Arthur covered a multitude of duties and, indeed, sins!

5
Mimizan – the Desire for Dollars

Once into the New Year, the days seemed to race by and it became increasingly obvious that the buildings at Derrinstown would not be even half finished by 16 March. I was becoming more and more frustrated. It was all very well the Duke decreeing that the cattle had to be on the farm by the spring, but it was equally obvious that he had no idea what was involved, for he had not the knowledge, nor had he considered the practicalities of his requirements.

With the possible problems that might occur in mind and the realization that if anything went wrong I would be the one to 'carry the can', I again consulted George Ridley. Was there any point in appealing to the Duke to delay the shipment? His answer was immediate. "None. A complete waste of time." He went on to suggest that I approach Sisks with a view to working three shifts every twenty-four hours. I contacted Michael O'Driscoll and informed him of the Chief Agent's proposition.

To begin with he laughed and, I think, doubted my sanity. "What's the rush?" However, when he realized I was deadly serious, he said he'd see what could be arranged. In due course he came back to me and said he thought he had enough skilled men to work two shifts, three was out of the question, but there was one major problem – the site would have to be floodlit and the nearest mains electricity was over two miles away! We were in the throes of installing two large generators which should have been operational long before Christmas, but there always seemed to be some delay or excuse as to why they were not.

The English firm, Pillingers, carrying out the installation

had only one competent and trustworthy fitter in Ireland and he had been instructed to oversee about four jobs at the same time! The result was that he was rushing hither and thither and getting nowhere. A most generous tip worked wonders – we had light within a week! At last we were getting somewhere. Michael O'Driscoll contacted me and said he had all the men he required for a second shift, except a foreman. He couldn't find a suitable man anywhere. However, there was one possibility, Paddy Casey, the foreman already in charge on the site, was prepared to work two shifts a day, six days a week, providing he was paid time and a half for all the hours he put in. What did I think?

By this time any solution was acceptable. However, as Ridley had made the original agreement with Sisks that the job should be done on a time and materials basis, I thought I'd better consult him. He fully approved. Get the buildings up whatever the cost! The Duke wanted his Shorthorns in Ireland. Further, George said I could expend up to £2,000 as 'sweeteners' to Paddy, or any of his helpers I thought worthy of a handout. As it turned out bribes were not necessary. I gave two £25 tips to an enraptured Paddy and that was all. Money was flowing into his home in a way he would never have dreamed possible, for, apart from himself, he had several members of his family employed on the site. No further incentive was required to obtain the maximum effort from him.

Had I had a different approach to life and other people's property, like some who worked for the Duke, I could have added £1,950 to my bank account without any difficulty – nearly two years' salary!

It was around this time that I started to see Ikey Bell on a very regular basis. He had rented a house from the Duke of Devonshire's Lismore Estates so that he could be near his old friend Benny when he visited Fort William. It was also around this time that I received a somewhat mystifying message from 'The Owner' via George Ridley. I was to draw £1,000 in cash from one of the Irish Accounts – apparently it did not matter which one – and hand it over to Ikey. I asked George what it was to be charged to in the books. I was told it was to be shown as a cash withdrawal by me and that was all. I didn't like it, it was too ambiguous, but again it was a case of 'mine not to reason why' and so I did as I was instructed.

When I handed over the cash to Ikey I quickly learned the reason. The Duke, like everyone else in Great Britain, was strictly limited as to the amount of money he could take out of the country for personal use, the only exception being to Eire. I forget exactly how much one was allowed, I seem to remember it was not more than £5 – not a lot of use to the Duke of Westminster!

Ikey, on the other hand, was an American citizen, subject to no such restrictions and his income came in dollars from the States. At their last meeting Bend Or told Ikey how anxious he was to go to France to his property outside the small town of Mimizan, situated on the coast some forty miles south of Bordeaux. Many years prior to the war the Duke had been a guest at a wild boar hunt in the area. He had been so taken by the wild and varied nature of the countryside that he immediately decided to buy some land, build a house, together with large stables and hound kennels, and start his own pack of boar hounds. For once, the house was not to be on a grand scale and, in the minimum of time, a hunting lodge, Château Woolsack, was built.

The actual building of it was, in itself, something of an achievement, for the approach to the site was via almost inaccessible forest roads. In 1947 the original château was gutted by fire, however, a timber annexe, which had been built subsequently to accommodate guests, remained. It was this that Bend Or was so anxious to visit and which currency restrictions made virtually impossible. He could not even send money to his trusted housekeeper, Thérèse Deleste, who had looked after his interests so well during the German occupation. Prior to their arrival she had buried many valuables in the forest – all were recovered safely at the end of the war.

Ikey, ever anxious to assist his friend, suggested that Bend Or should pay him sterling in Ireland and he, Ikey, would have dollars (most welcome in any European country) sent to France. It is probable that neither realized that to do this was strictly illegal, at least as far as the Duke was concerned – being found guilty of illegal currency dealing could result in a lengthy prison sentence.

George McVeagh warned Ridley as to the possible consequences and although Ridley tried to get him involved, he flatly refused to have anything to do with it, advising George to follow his lead. The latter laughed at him and simply said what Bend Or wanted he must have. I, too, voiced my unease at any involvement, but it was quickly made very clear to me that if I wished to retain my job, then quite simply I did what I was told, which was to cash a cheque for whatever sum was named by the Duke and deliver it to Ikey. Grudgingly I agreed, but on the understanding that I received these instructions from Ridley in writing. To this, equally grudgingly, he agreed.

All was well until a new clerk, from the firm who did the audit, demanded an explanation for the cash withdrawals. I had been briefed, in the event of this happening, simply to say I was not at liberty to say. He was a rather obnoxious young man and started making innuendos about 'feathering nests' and 'hands in tills'. I'd had enough. I phoned Ridley and said that what the Duke and Ikey Bell got up to was entirely their business, but I was not having my name besmirched and would have no part in these illicit transactions. I was quickly told I would do what I was told – that is if I knew what was good for me. However, with feelings of considerable trepidation I stuck to my guns. Ridley was not pleased, but the outcome was that I quickly received the following letter, dated 15 December 1950, and which I still have:

> "My agent in Ireland, M. F. Twist, has received the sum of £27,930 (Twenty-seven thousand, nine hundred and thirty pounds) from me during the course of the past two or three years and I hereby confirm that Twist has expended this sum on my behalf and in accordance with my personal instructions. Westminster."

End of story, as far as the Irish agricultural estate accounts were concerned, for which I was truly grateful, but not the end of Bend Or's arrangement with Ikey. The London office now became the source of sterling. Low denomination notes were collected from the Pimlico rents office and, various couriers, but never the Duke, transported them to Ikey. Ikey told me towards the latter part of his life that the Duke's insistence on having dollars nearly beggared him.

'The Owner' was never happier than when at Mimizan, or the even more remote Lochmore Lodge, his residence on the Reay Forest Estates in Sutherlandshire. It was a wild, magnificent area, situated south of Cape Wrath. One of its main attractions for the Duke was the River Laxford, which ranked amongst the finest salmon rivers in the British Isles. It seemed that salmon fishing was one of the Duke's lasting interests. Ikey always claimed that, even as a young man, fishing came very high on Bend Or's list of popular pursuits, with a ranking nearly comparable to that for the fairer sex!

Whilst I never visited Mimizan, I did visit Lochmore and my wife, Cynthia, and I stayed with George and Mary Ridley at Gobernuisgach, a property that adjoined the Duke's original estate and which had been purchased in 1950 as an agricultural/forestry investment. Its addition must have brought the area of the Duke's Sutherlandshire estate up to something in the region of 1000 square miles!

If Lochmore Lodge was remote, then Gobernuisgach was remoter still! When we stayed there I had given up smoking, but not so Cynthia. She ran out of cigarettes so, following George's instructions on to how to get to the nearest shop, we set off to replenish supplies. By the time we returned we had motored 72 miles! To this day I do not know if Ridley deliberately sent us off on a 'wild goose chase' or whether it really was the nearest place to buy a packet of cigarettes.

Certainly Gobernuisgach was isolated. After leaving the main road it took some twenty to thirty minutes along a rough mountain track to reach the lodge. The latter was single line traffic, with passing places every few hundred yards! It always intrigued me that the house had ever been built in the first place. Apparently it owed its existence to the fact that Queen Victoria and Prince Albert wanted somewhere quiet to stay to go deer stalking. The nearest railway station was, if I remember correctly, Lairg, some seventy or more miles away. Goberniusgach was difficult enough to reach by motor car, what it must have been like in the days of horse-drawn vehicles is almost beyond comprehension.

However, it was not difficult to understand the Duke's love for his Scottish estate. Apart from the scenery, the wildlife was riveting. In the two weeks I was there I saw golden eagles every day. On one occasion, when driving down to the Gobernuisgach river, a pair passed within thirty yards of me – a magnificent sight as they glided on the wind only feet off the ground, following a hind with a very late and sickly looking calf.

Driving back to Gobernuisgach Lodge of an evening, having spent the day fishing Loch Stack, the red deer coming down off the mountains to drink from the burn in the valley provided a quite splendid spectacle – one that I will remember all my life.

Apart from the wild unspoilt grandeur that so appealed to him, the Duke also had a great affinity with those who worked on his estate. Proud, loyal retainers who, through his common touch and enthusiasm for their rugged land, commanded their respect and affection. He was in fact most comfortable and at ease with unsophisticated and unpretentious folk.

I well remember the pleasure he derived, when at Fort William, from having some of the locals to lunch or dinner. Comparatively simple people who amused him and were not continually toadying or trying to get something from him. He was really, in spite of his wealth and position, 'of the people'. He gave an annual Gillies Ball at Lochmore. On one occasion, as his guests were leaving, he turned to a friend and said, "If I could have such people to dine every night of the year, I would be a very happy man".

Conversely, he could quickly become bored and irritated by people. I remember once staying the night at Fort William when the Duke was there. Sacheverell Sitwell was a guest and had been for several days. When I arrived I found the Duke, normally so charming, in foul mood. Ikey and his wife, Dolly, came to dinner that night. When the ladies had left us men to our cigars and port, the conversation became very strained. Suddenly the Duke stood up.

"Come on, we'll join the ladies."

When we reached the hall Sitwell said, "I'm just going along to the toilet." I heard 'The Owner' positively snort, then he turned to Ikey.

"Extraordinary bloody fellow." With that he switched on the porch light, opened the front door, stepped out onto the drive and proceeded to have a pee! Ikey joined him. Not wishing to be considered 'an extraordinary bloody fellow', I eased into the shadows and made up the tripartite.

I left the following morning to go to Bruree long before the Duke had risen from his bed. That evening I had a phone call from Ikey. The Duke had returned to England. He'd had enough of his 'friend' Sitwell!

Ikey once told me that, before the war, Bend Or used to have vast house parties for Chester Races. In one room there was always a barrel of beer. Guests were told to help themselves if they felt thirsty. The Duke would insist that Ikey should wait up with him until everyone had gone to bed. Then 'The Owner' would prowl through the rooms commenting on the amount of drink that was left, cigars just lit and virtually left unsmoked. The thing, according to Ikey, that seemed to annoy him most was if anyone left some beer. One night they came upon a full tankard, untouched and by then very flat. The Duke was furious and tried to make Ikey drink it. He refused. The Duke departed to bed in a huff. The next morning Ikey found his friend Bend Or had left, leaving the house party to entertain themselves!

George Ridley's plan – ' Operation Death Duties' – started to materialize at the end of 1947, when the Whinfell Estate in Cumberland was purchased. Around the same time Langshaw Rowland joined the Duke's staff, to become Director of Woodlands. He'd had his own forestry and timber business which he had operated largely from the Eaton Estate sawmill at Belgrave. Langshaw had taken a lease on this some years previously and was very much 'a name' in forestry – so much so that he was subsequently elected President of the Royal Forestry Society. George Ridley arranged to buy Langshaw out, for a very handsome figure, and appointed him to the job he was to do with such drive and expertise over the next six to seven years. During that time Langshaw was responsible for planting an area of somewhere between 15,000 and 20,000 acres, plus developing and overseeing a thriving timber business.

Nineteen forty-eight saw further additions to the Duke's agricultural properties with the purchase of the Brancepeth and Ketteringham Estates. Ridley was jubilant. Like with many great men, success acted as a spur. He became more ambitious, more confident, more certain of his infallibility, more determined than ever to save the Grosvenor millions. His thoughts turned to investments outside Great Britain, but this was a different game altogether. This was one that needed Treasury approval.

People in high places were becoming aware of the fact that vast sums were being invested in such a way that much of the Grosvenor fortune would slip through their fingers when the Duke died. Therefore, they were not inclined to look with favour upon any scheme that might remove part of the Westminster fortune from within their orbit. This had to be a case, as Bill Bryan put it, of 'softly, softly catchee monkey'. Ridley appreciated this, but time was not on his side. In spite of this he had to take it and try and win over the opposition – not an easy task with a Labour Government in power which was openly hostile towards the nobility. Ursula and Stephen Vernon attended a party in Mayfair, at which Aneurin Bevan was present. Ursie told me on her return to Bruree what a delightful man he was, and so amusing!

"Do you know, Michael, he actually said he'd like to see me and my father barefoot begging in the gutter. Did you ever hear anything so hilarious!"

March the sixteenth seemed to approach at a quite alarming rate, whilst the buildings at Derrinstown appeared to advance at a snail's pace. Would Sisks have them ready in time? It was obvious they would not. I, therefore, had to plan accordingly. I asked Sisks to concentrate on completing the renovation of the existing cow-byre, and the finalization of the food store and the calf-house. If these were ready we could probably cope. It was during these anxious weeks that I was approached by the owner of the adjoining farm – Donaghstown. 'Would His Grace be interested in buying it?' I showed, I hope, little interest. It was exactly what we needed, for the acreage at Derrinstown was certainly not sufficient to accommodate the number of Shorthorns that the Duke now thought he'd like in Ireland, and it certainly was not enough to make it a viable proposition. The acquisition of Donaghstown would double the acreage. I enquired what was the asking price? Without batting an eye the owner went into a long spiel as to the wonders of the land, the best in Co. Kildare, then quite solemnly asked me for £25,000 – nearly three times the market value. Several weeks, and many hundreds of words later, I bought it for £9,000!

On 19 February, a Saturday, I crossed to England on the night boat, accompanied by Dick Powley, to make the final check and assist with the despatch of thirty-five Shorthorn females and one bull to the Glasgow Quarantine Station. They left on the Sunday afternoon, by special train, from Waverton station. I have seldom been colder! Dick and I caught the night train from Crewe to Glasgow, arriving in time to see the herd safely ensconced in what was to be their home for the next three weeks. Dick's younger brother, Anthony, a very experienced herdsman, and another young lad by the name of Wolfe, were to stay with the herd while it was in quarantine. Nothing was to be left to chance. Having seen them all safely in and well bedded down, Dick and I took a taxi to the airport and caught the plane back to Dublin.

By this time I had an office in the city and a most able secretary, Honor Reveille. After a quick lunch, I made my way to the office to check on what had been happening in my absence, greatly hoping there would be nothing too urgent. I was completely exhausted, for I had hardly slept for the last two nights. I was greeted by a worried looking Mrs Reveille.

"Thank goodness you've called in, Mr Twist. Richard Chapman has just been on the phone. His Grace would like to see you at Eaton this evening, preferably in time for dinner. You are to stay the night."

I couldn't believe it. I had been on the estate the whole of the previous day. He knew I was there. Why couldn't he have sent for me then? I walked silently into my office. I was too tired to give vent to my feelings. An anxious-looking Honor Reveille followed me in.

"You look exhausted." Then hesitantly added, "I've booked you on the 3.45pm plane to Liverpool – just in case."

"No, get Mr Ridley on the phone for me." Fortunately George was in the estate office at Eaton. He was just about to leave for The Hall to see the Duke. I explained the situation and that I was really too drained of energy to fly back to England that afternoon unless it was something desperately urgent.

"Don't worry. I'll be talking to the Duke within the next quarter of an hour. If he insists on seeing you I'll get Richard to phone at once, otherwise forget it."

I heard nothing. George phoned just as I was about to leave my office to say all was well. The Duke just wanted to know if his cattle had arrived safely in Glasgow. Two minutes, or less, on the phone would have answered his query, but His Grace didn't like using the telephone, so it was easier, from his point of view, to have an employee come to him. In all the time I worked for the Duke I only ever spoke to him twice on the phone.

The 16 March came all too quickly. A bitterly cold day, but at least it was dry. It was just after 7.00am as I stood in what seemed like arctic conditions on the North Wall, Dublin, watching the ship berth. Seven lorries from the C.I.E., the Irish government-owned transport company, were lined up ready on the dock to take their much-publicised cargo to Maynooth. Members of the press were present, as were three Garda Síochána – a Superintendent and two constables. The former was a cheerful individual, a native of Co. Roscommon and a keen shooting man. He remarked how appropriate it was that the first full day the Duke's cows would be in Ireland would be St Patrick's Day – 17 March.

At last the ship was moored and the unloading ramp in place. After some five minutes, four dockers detached themselves from a group of ten, who had been standing idly by. They sauntered off into the nether regions of the ship – followed by Dick. Some minutes later the dockers reappeared, each leading one of the famous Eaton Shorthorns, all suitably attired in monogrammed rugs, leather head collars with shining brass buckles and white lead ropes. The four were closely followed by Dick, leading yet another of the consignment. As he appeared one of the remaining dockers ran forward and stood in front of Dick, holding up his hand.

"Begob, is you tryin' to steal our jobs? I'm tellin' you we'll have none o' t'at. Come on boys – strike!"

To my horror the quartet immediately dropped the lead ropes. Four of the Duke's prized cows were adrift on Dublin quay! But the arm-of-the-law was quick. The Superintendent grabbed one, a garda another and two of the C.I.E. drivers made sure the remaining two did not set out on an unscheduled tour of the city. I could see Dick's colour mounting and, with it, his temper. I stepped hastily forward to where the foreman docker stood.

"Now, don't get all worked up. No-one is trying to take your job, at least none of us." The man stood glowering and muttering profanities. I reached for my wallet and took out a £1 note and nine 10 shilling ones.

"Here, you and your men have a drink with His Grace." A smile spread across the troublemaker's face.

"By the hokey an' aren't you th' gentleman, an' I'll flatten anyone who says different, so I will. Come on lads, don't keep the gentleman waitin'."

The thirty-five females came off the ship with alacrity, then there was a pause – no bull. The foreman appeared, looking slightly sheepish. He walked over to where I stood.

"Himself, below, is not of a mind to leave the boat. Would t'is gentleman give a hand?" As he said this he jerked a thumb in the direction of Dick. I saw the latter was about to suffer a verbal explosion, so hastily intervened.

"Of course, no problem." I nodded at Dick, who once more departed into the bowels of the ship. Shortly he returned leading the bull, very much on his toes and bellowing at one and all.

The consignment arrived at Derrinstown, to be unloaded

amidst piles of ballast, stacks of timber and clattering concrete mixers. When all were safely housed, Dick and I made a careful inspection of the thirty-six animals. All seemed well and none the worse for their journey. I went into the house, now occupied by Dick and his family. We'd at last got the telephone connected. I rang Honor Reveille and told her to despatch a pre-arranged telegram to the Duke, telling him his cattle had arrived safely.

It was one evening in mid-April that Ridley phoned me to say that the Duke and Duchess were crossing to Ireland that night. 'The Owner' wished me to meet them at the Shelbourne, the next day, for lunch; after which the Duke wanted to go out to Derrinstown to see his herd. I arrived at the Shelbourne in good time. The first person I saw as I entered the hotel was Jim Willoughby, the chauffeur from Fort William. After a few minutes chat, I said I assumed that he would follow me out to the farm, but, nevertheless, gave him detailed instructions how to get there in case we were parted in the traffic leaving the city.

I had only just seated myself in the lounge when the Duke and Duchess entered. The former seemed in cracking form and, after a quick drink, we went in for lunch – a most enjoyable meal from every aspect. Little was said about the Irish estates or the herd. The Duke was very preoccupied with the thought that Ikey Bell was being very mean with his dollars and that he, the Duke, was anxious to organize a trip to Norway to fish the River Alta for salmon.

He had gone there for many years prior to the war. He used to go in his yacht, taking a select and favoured party with him. In the mid-twenties one night's catch was something in excess of thirty salmon, averaging close on 25 lbs each. He was thirsting for the chance to try and renew the experience. Bend Or was not a man who spoke in whispers! I looked anxiously around as he kept on about Ikey and dollars. He had, I gathered, been told that his and Ikey's little arrangement was strictly contrary to law. At last I steered him off the subject and suggested that Willoughby should follow me out to Maynooth.

"No, you come with us. We can talk." With that he stood up and prepared to leave the dining room. As we left, Peter the head waiter touched me on the arm and discreetly asked if I'd sign the bill. I obliged. The Duke, I was to learn, seldom carried money. All accounts were sent to his nearest office for settlement. Nor, so it seemed, did he ever personally tip waiters or anyone else who had been of service, this was left to senior members of his staff to deal with, but they were never forgotten for the Duke was a most generous man over such matters. At Christmas I received instructions to tip certain members of the staff at the Shelbourne. The head waiter received £50, his second-in-command and the wine waiter £25 each and the hall porter the same – a great deal of money in those days! The Duke always received excellent service, so, I might add, did I!

We all climbed into the vast V8 Ford, which was kept at Fort William, and headed for Derrinstown. We quickly reached our destination. The farmyard was a long way from completion. Jim Willoughby manoeuvred the car up the rough track, to a recently concreted area beyond the house. We got out and I led the way to the entrance of the cow-byre, where Dick was waiting for us. He had brought the herd in from the fields early. They were spotless. All had been brushed until their coats positively shone, they were bedded up to their hocks in the best and cleanest of wheat straw – in fact there wasn't a cowpat in sight! The Duke glanced down the byre, he didn't enter. He looked around the yard where Sisk's men were all hard at work. They had been told not to gawp, even if they hadn't seen a real live duke before!

"Very good, Twist. Looks a bit like a bloody prison – all iron bars and concrete. Come on Nance, think we'll get on to the Fort."

The Duchess turned to him. "What about Mr Twist, how's he going to get back to Dublin?"

"Oh, he'll be all right. Won't you Twist?"

I assured him that I would. I bid him and the Duchess farewell, it had at most been four minutes since we had driven into the yard. As I watched the car bump its way down the track to the road, I wondered why Paddy Casey had worked 96 hours a week for nearly two months. It also left me wondering why we had all been rushing around since the previous November to be ready for the moment now fleetingly gone.

The Duke only visited Derrinstown on one more occasion, that was in 1949, but more about that later.

6
An Igenious Legal Fiddle

Magnificent pedigree Shorthorns were good publicity in an agricultural country but tax evasion was still the name of the game. To someone like the Duke of Westminster the Irish tax laws applicable to agriculture were a boon, although I doubt if he personally was aware of the fact. However, some of us were and we began exploring ways to obtain the maximum benefits for His Grace.

When trying to appreciate the value of these laws, one must relate the value of money at the time about which I write, the late 1940s and early 50s, to that of the present. For example a farm worker in Ireland in the late 1940s received wages of approximately £2 and 10 shillings per week, (250p). The same worker today would receive well in excess of £100. A rough guideline would be £1000 then equals £40,000 now.

One of 'The Owner's' great advantages was that he was a dual resident. Losses in Ireland could be offset against tax liability in Great Britain and this was dealt with through the Conjoint Office. A most admirable institution as far as the Irish were concerned, responsible for bringing many thousands of pounds into the Government coffers. A most popular arrangement with the Irish revenue authorities! Apart from being able to carry out improvements and developments against British tax, there were a number of other advantages.

The revenue authorities agreed that His Grace was a double resident, the effect of this decision was to cause liability for tax to arise in each country on the full income for each year. However, in accordance with the agreement between the two countries embodied in the Finance Acts of

1926 and 1928 double taxation relief was granted in each country, the effect of which reduced the rate of tax to such a sum as the taxpayer would have to meet if resident in that country in which the higher rate prevailed.

However, the occupation of land in Ireland was dealt with under Schedule B. Under this Schedule the Revenue sought to assess profits from husbandry. The measure of liability was taken to be the Poor Law Valuation. Thus, the maximum assessment which a taxpayer in Ireland was called upon to meet, in respect of farming profits, was the amount of the Poor Law Valuation – normally an insignificant amount. If, on the other hand, a taxpayer was able to prove that his farming operations had resulted in a loss, then he could claim to have the amount of this loss set off against any other income he might have. The beauty of this Schedule was that notwithstanding any such claim the taxpayer could, if he so desired, revert to the valuation basis in the following year. Further, if profit was received from the breeding and sale of horses, or from fees received for the services of a stallion on the lands, it was deemed to arise from the occupation of land and the measure of tax liability on a stud farm was wholly exhausted by the Schedule B Assessment. It was, for the Duke, a case of heads I win tails you lose.

In 1948 and 1949 the Schedule B Assessment on the Bruree Stud was £424. Had the stud been properly managed by Stephen Vernon it could have been a gold mine, but it was not, for a number of the mares were of medium to poor breeding, several being retained through sentiment rather than financial worth. A close friend of mine in Co. Kildare sold his yearlings in 1952 at the Doncaster Sales for £44,500 – his tax liability, based on the Poor Law Valuation of his stud, was £315! Alas, the Duke would not make the necessary capital available for the purchase of brood mares of the highest calibre and firmly closed the door on what could have been a most lucrative investment. However, other opportunities to gain from such salutary tax laws began to dawn.

In January 1948 the Duke made his Irish will, of which I received a copy. He bequeathed all his lands, together with the buildings thereon, the bloodstock, pedigree herds, all other livestock and farm machinery to the Duchess, together with household effects – in fact the lot! There were two wishes that the Duke expressed in the latter part of the will. Firstly, that the Duchess should retain the herds and bloodstock on the various holdings in Ireland at the time of this death. Secondly, that she should, as far as possible, retain in her employment all employees usually employed in Ireland at that time. 'As far as possible' was to prove a crucial phrase. The Duke's kind and generous thoughts were never implemented.

However, to return to happier days. It was fine willing the properties to the Duchess, but to become a gift *inter vivos*, that is free of death duties, the Duke would have to live another five years. That might not happen. There had to be a way of making the properties over to the Duchess to safeguard the future. Further, if it could be done in such a way as to benefit the Duke's tax position, so much the better. I kept turning the problem over in my mind. I was sure the answer lay in the Duchess buying the properties, but how? Eventually I consulted Willie Sandys, senior partner of Griffin Lynch, the Dublin accountants who had recently been appointed to act for the Duke in Ireland.

Willie had a brilliant brain and loved to pit his wits against the revenue authorities. Having told him what was in my mind he went off to think about it. Several weeks passed before he contacted me. He telephoned me one day to say he thought he had the answer. He went on to tell me that he had worked out a scheme which he was sure would achieve not only the transfer of the properties, livestock and equipment to the Duchess, but would also be beneficial to the Duke, bearing in mind that, from an income and surtax point of view, the Duke and Duchess were as one. Willie asked me to set up a meeting as soon as possible with George McVeagh. This I did.

Several days later, after lunch at the Shelbourne, we walked round to the office I now had in Merrion Square, situated on the second floor above the Australian Embassy. Willie outlined his plan. It was ingenious, but remarkably simple. I wondered why I hadn't thought of it.

To summarize, firstly, a limited company had to form under the Company Act of 1908 to 1924. The Duchess would hold ninety-eight per cent of the shares. There would be two other nominees, each holding one share. The Duchess would receive a gift from the Duke for however much was required, it transpired that it was £40,000. She would use this sum to subscribe for the share capital of the company. Willie suggested that she would actually pay £10,000 and make a loan to the company of £30,000. The company would then purchase the properties from the Duke, with the money already given by him to the Duchess. This would come back to him as 'real' money, that is to say money not subject to income tax. The original loan would be put through the Head Office (London) books as a gift. Care, Willie insisted, should be taken to have a valuation of all the property and stock carried out by a reputable firm of valuers.

This was subsequently done and a figure of £36,025 was agreed. In view of the vast amount of money already spent on the properties it was an incredibly low figure. But one that was never disputed by 'the powers that be'.

The next step was for the Duchess to become the tenant of the company. Whilst she was the main shareholder in the company, in law she and it were two distinct entities. A rent would be charged, again assessed by a valuer. This was, in round figures, agreed at £10,000. As the prime objective on the Irish farms at this stage was to improve the properties and show as big a loss as possible, the payment of rent would up the Duke's claim for tax rebate by this sum. No small amount in those days. The company would be subject to a tax liability, the Schedule A assessment on the properties, namely the Poor Law Valuation plus twenty-five per cent. A minimal amount compared with what was to be gained. The majority of the rental received would go towards paying off the loan to the company, which had been made by the Duchess!

It was brilliant. I asked Willie what would happen when the loan was paid of? He had the answer ready. When this happened he advised that the balance, standing to credit in the revenue account, should be capitalised and shares issued in respect of this sum. It all seemed too good to be true. I asked Willie if he really thought the revenue authorities would wear it? He smiled broadly.

"Yes, I saw the head of the Department this morning. He's a good friend of mine."

"What did he say?"

"Oh, that it was a most ingenious fiddle, but perfectly legal. He added that if it kept His Grace happy, fine, no one in his department would object. Apparently, thanks to the Conjoint Office, the Duke pays more income tax than anyone else in the country. In fact, I think he said, the Duke contributes about one twelfth of the total revenue derived from this source."

We talked it through again, George and I both trying to find faults with the plan – we couldn't. I turned to George.

"How soon can you set up a company once we get the go ahead from the Duke?"

"Quite quickly. There shouldn't be any trouble, but we do need a name."

I thought for a moment. "How about 'Munster & Leinster Estates'? All the properties are within the two provinces."

The meeting broke up, with it being left to me to contact George Ridley. When I phoned him later that afternoon he was delighted with the idea and said he'd put it to the Duke as soon as he had it all in writing. The Duke approved. It seemed as though he was getting a real taste for the tax rebate game!

All went well, that is until we reached the stage of

advertising the proposed name for the company in the national press. An objection to the name was lodged by the Munster & Leinster Bank. They did not know who was behind the company and were afraid the latter might obtain credit it couldn't afford, due to people believing it was connected to the bank. The bank, incidentally, was quite a small one with a capital of some four and a half million. George McVeagh and I thought it a great joke – the Duke could buy the bank up out of the petty cash!

I left it to George to straighten the matter out. It so happened that Their Graces were at Fort William, and I was summoned to their presence. As frequently happened, it was at very short notice and I had one hell of a rush to motor the 146 miles in time for lunch. 'The Owner' seemed in great form and I was warmly received, except by Dringalo the dachshund, who had a go at my ankle, much to the Duke's amusement. There were only the three of us and just as we started our main course the Duke turned to me.

"How's this company coming along?"

Laughing, I told him about the bank's objection to the name. It was immediately obvious that His Grace did not think it at all funny.

"Oh, oh! Well I rather like that name. Tell you what, you go and ring up the chairman of this bank and ask him what he'll take for it. Now." He turned to John Lynch, the resident butler. "Take Mr Twist's lunch and keep it warm for him. Twist you go and ring this fellow up right away." The Duchess intervened. "Oh let him finish his lunch in peace, Benny." But I was already on my way. Fortunately, I knew the chairman, Colonel Charlie O'Kelly. He lived not far from Maynooth and I had been dining with him only a few nights before. I also knew he was a member of the Kildare Street Club, *the* club in Ireland and that he normally lunched there. I was lucky; he'd just arrived. He came to the phone and didn't sound in very good form. Perhaps he was anxious to have his lunch, so was I. I decided not to waste time in

The 2nd Duke of Westminster. Picture courtesy The Times © 1948.

View of the farmyard at Derrinstown on 17 March 1948, the day the herd arrived.

The fleet of lorries bringing the Dairy Shorthorns to Derrinstown, Maynooth, Co. Kildare.

The entrance to Derrinstown, June 1948.

Part of the finished farmyard at Derrinstown, June 1948.

Left: The chandelier which caused so much extra work.

Right: Dairy Shorthorn cow, Holmscales Annetta 20th. The Supreme Champion Shorthorn (Beef and Dairy), the Royal Dublin Society Spring Show 1949. The only time this was won by a Dairy Shorthorn.

Below: Fort William House.

Below: George Ridley and the author at the sale of tuberculosis-tested Shorthorn heifers brought over from Ireland as replacements for those that failed the Tuberculin Test on the Eaton Estate.

STATION—LISMORE
TEL.—LISMORE 7

Fort William,
Glencairn,
Co. Waterford,
Ireland.

15th Dec. 1950

My Agent in Ireland, M. F. Twist, has received the sum of £27.930 (twenty seven thousand nine hundred and thirty Pounds) from me during the course of the past two or three years and I hereby confirm that Twist has expended this sum on my behalf and in accordance with my personal instructions.

Windsor.

A copy of the letter to the author from the Duke, dated 15 December 1950.

Lady Ursula Vernon, the Duke's eldest daughter, and her husband, Major Stephen Vernon, at the author's wedding.

Above: Derek Turner, Bill Bryan and the author at a livestock sale.

Ikey Bell chatting with George Ridley at the author's wedding.

Bryanstown

Eaton Fragrance 6th, sold for 560 guineas with her heifer calf which sold for 250 Guineas – a record price in Ireland – when the herd was sold five months after the death of the Duke.

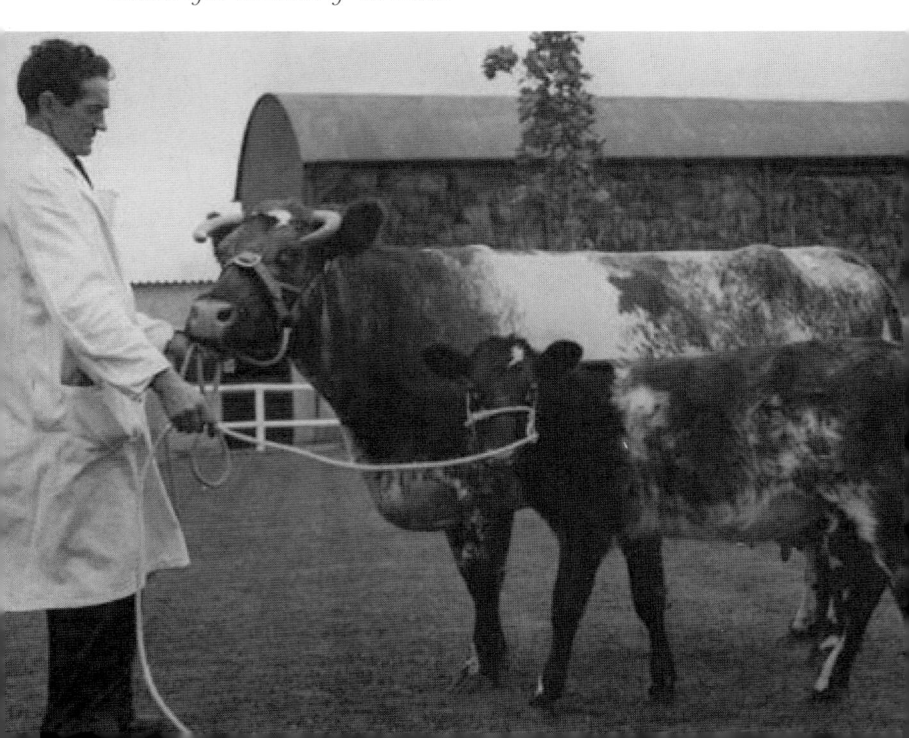

preliminary small talk and came straight to the point.

"Charlie, I'm with the Duke at Lismore. He has taken great exception to your objecting to the name of his new company, Munster & Leinster Estates. He says he's going to have the name, whether you like it or not and has instructed me to find out what you'll take for your bank." There was complete and utter silence. "Are you there?"

"Yes. Have you been drinking Michael, or is this some sort of joke that I don't understand?"

"The answer to your question is neither. I assure you that His Grace is absolutely serious."

There was silence again for a minute and then he started to laugh, finally he said, "I don't know anything about this, but I will do as soon as I get back to the bank. In the meantime please tell His Grace that I have no desire to sell the bank, even if I could and that he can certainly have the name for his company. You might like to suggest to him that as I've been so co-operative, he puts a little business our way."

So Munster & Leinster Estates came into being without further fuss. I must say I was somewhat relieved. I didn't really want a bank added to my responsibilities!

It seemed that the Duke's affairs, both agricultural and personal, went from the sublime to the ridiculous. The Duke's personal affairs covered a wide spectrum, sometimes amusing, at other times annoying and a complete waste of time. One such incident followed the Duke's next visit to Lismore. He was only there for about three days and I saw him the afternoon before he left. Immediately on his return to Eaton he sent for Bill Bryan – very urgent. The problem? The Duke's loo at the Fort.

Both he and the Duchess had magnificent carved oak thrones, complete with armrests and high backs surmounted by coronets, encasing the pans of their toilets. They were undoubtedly magnificent works of art, made by a carpenter in Lismore. It appeared that the Duke thought the seat of his was not as smooth as it had been. He suggested that perhaps one of the maids might have dropped something on it. Anyway, I was to leave whatever I was doing, go to Fort William immediately, investigate and, if necessary, have the seat sandpapered and polished! Bill gave a laugh and continued. "I think 'The Owner' would like you to try it out." My reply is best left unrecorded. I mean to say, *honi soit qui mal y pense* is all very well, but there are limits!

It was early spring when the Duke and Duchess once again decided to visit Ireland. Actually it was not many weeks after the 'smoothing of the throne' episode. I received a message that His Grace would like me to meet him at the Shelbourne for lunch and, afterwards, he wished to visit Derrinstown. I was delighted. Things were looking really well there and we were preparing a team of Shorthorns to be exhibited at the Royal Dublin Society's Spring Show, Ireland's premier agricultural event.

The day the Duke arrived it was both cold and wet. Nevertheless, His Grace seemed in excellent form, exuding charm as he so frequently did. I was quickly to learn that things were going well regarding his planned trip to Norway, as I have already said, a favourite stamping ground of his for many years before the war. He was like a schoolboy about to go on holiday. Quite obviously he was thrilled at the thought of introducing his beloved Nancy to the excitements and thrills of the River Alta. There was only one problem, the trip would have to be courtesy of Ikey.

Salmon fishing, even in the 40s, was not cheap. Dollars were urgently needed! That was the main consideration behind the current visit to Ireland. Apparently Ikey was not being as co-operative as the Duke felt he should be and was not keen to supply more dollars than were needed for the regular payments now going to France. In simple language, Bend Or had come to twist his friend's arm!

Lunch over, we set off for Maynooth. At his request I again travelled with the Duke. The Duchess must have seen a slight look of misgiving cross my face, for she assured me that they would be returning to Dublin. They were staying at the Shelbourne overnight and she had some shopping she wished to do before they went on to Fort William. Then, with a definite twinkle in her eye, she added "At least that's the plan at the moment."

Just outside Maynooth we passed Carton, for many years the family seat of the Duke of Leinster. It had recently been sold to Lord Brocket, a wealthy brewer amongst many other things. I mentioned that Carton had been sold and, in passing, that there was shortly to be a big auction of the contents lasting several days,. I was surprised at the interest this casual remark aroused in the Duke. "Haven't stayed there since before the Great War. Lovely place. At least it used to be. Wish I'd known it was coming up for sale, I might have bought it. You should have told me Twist."

I had told Ridley, but he hadn't been interested. He'd said it was not the type of investment required.

We drove up the new, tree-lined, concrete road into the yard at Derrinstown. The rain was lashing down; it couldn't have been a worse afternoon. It was with some reluctance that the Duke got out of the car. Even though Jim Willoughby, the chauffeur, had, on my instructions, brought the car to a halt under the covered walk that led from the cow-byre to the dairy. The Duke looked around.

"That's better. Not so much like a bloody prison. Not so many iron bars." He moved to just inside the entrance to the byre where Dick Powley was waiting. He greeted Dick warmly and looked down the shed. The tubular steel partitions for the stalls were clearly visible.

"Hmmm, spoke to soon. Still iron bars everywhere. Come on, let's go and look round Carton." He turned and moved back towards the car. I think the Duchess noted the look of acute disappointment on Dick's face, for she smiled at him and said.

"Never mind, Powley, another time, when it's a better day." But there never was another time. The Duke never again visited Derrinstown, or indeed any of the other Maynooth properties!

We drove up the potholed drive to the front of Carton. The rain had stopped and we all climbed out of the car. It looked cold and uninviting. The Duke moved towards the front door.

"Let's take a look round. See what they're selling."

I rang the front door bell, but no one came. As I rang again I could hear a bell, quite distinctly, ringing through the house, so I knew it was working. After a few more minutes, Jim Willoughby departed around the side of the house. I kept my finger firmly on the bell push. The Duke, quite obviously, was becoming irritated. He wasn't used to being kept waiting. Just then, through the large windows either side of the door, we all three saw Jim walking across the hall. The Duke grabbed the Duchess's arm.

"Come on Nance. Bloody fellow'll get us arrested for house breaking. Come on, quick."

He propelled the Duchess off down the drive at speed. Just as Jim opened the door, a red-faced caretaker came running up.

"What the hell's going on? Breaking into the house are you? If you don't go at once I'll send for the Garda."

I explained that we were with the Duke of Westminster and that he wanted to see what was going in the auction. As I talked I pulled out my wallet, extracted a fiver and handed it to the now mollified caretaker. I sent Jim off down the drive to retrieve the Duke and Duchess. When they entered the hall, the caretaker was all smiles. Bowing, he told the Duke to go ahead. He could take as long as he liked and that he, the caretaker, would be waiting in the hall when His Honour was ready to leave.

We set off at a brisk pace. There seemed to be a mass of heavy Victorian furniture and vast gilt-framed mirrors everywhere. It was obvious that the Duchess wanted to stop and examine some of the lots, but the Duke strode on, as though he had some definite goal in mind. At last we entered a small room, at least small compared with the ones we'd been hurrying through.

"Ah! The Chinese Room." The Duke turned to his wife. "Queen Victoria slept here." He looked around the room before moving over to the fireplace. He stood looking at the large mirror above it, with its ornate, beautifully carved gilt surround. It really was rather fine, but then so were a number of the other mirrors we'd passed. The Duke turned to me.

"Buy that, Twist." And off he went again. I looked at the Duchess.

"I wonder how much he wants to give for it?" As I spoke I wrote down the lot number, 608. "Most of the dealers in Great Britain and Ireland will be here. I'm sure there'll be very inflated prices." The Duchess called after the receding figure of her husband.

"Benny, Mr Twist wants to know how much you want to give for it. He says there'll be dealers here from all over the place. Prices are bound to be high." 'The Owner' stopped and turned.

"Well they've got to stop bidding sometime. Buy it." On he went. The Duchess, smiling, turned to me.

"You heard. Buy it."

It so happened that at the time the auction was to take place I had Terence Coffey, a most able chartered accountant now attached to the Duke's London office, coming for a three-day visit to Ireland. We were to set up a completely new set of books for the Irish estates. Far more important, in my estimation, than chasing around after a large, ornate mirror! However, the Duke had said buy it and that was that. I tried to put Coffey off, but it would be at least two months before he could possibly come if we didn't keep to our agreed plan. He was scheduled to visit all the estates to coordinate the accounts.

I delegated the buying of the mirror to Dick Powley, although I wasn't entirely happy in so doing. Should anything go wrong it would be my head that would be on the block! So there could be no mistake, I put my instructions in writing, the lot number and that he was to buy it whatever it made. Further, I went to Carton and showed Dick the mirror. Dick seemed unimpressed. He'd sooner have looked at a good cow!

"What do you think it will fetch?"

"I honestly don't know, Dick. It's really immaterial. I've made some enquiries from a couple of auctioneers in Dublin. They say these large gilt mirrors don't make a lot. £25 to £30, that sort of price. But, whatever it makes, you are to buy it."

The evening of the auction I was staying, together with Coffey, at The Dunraven Arms, Adare. An excellent small hotel, about half an hour's drive from Bruree. We'd had a tiring and difficult day discussing the stud accounts with Stephen Vernon, not the world's most brilliant businessman! He really didn't want to know and kept reiterating that the wellbeing of the Duke's bloodstock was his job, not accountancy. Feeling relaxed after an excellent dinner, I phoned Dick.

"Did you buy the mirror?"

"Yes."

Inwardly I gave sigh of relief. However competent Dick was, I hadn't been really happy delegating a direct order from the Duke – supposing something had gone wrong?

"What did you pay for it?" There was silence for a moment.

"A lot more than you said you thought it'd make. You did say I was to buy it, whatever it made?"

"Yes. How much?"

"£860... and just seconds after it had been knocked down to me a priest rushed in. He was in a frightful state; his car had broken down on his way from Co. Donegal. He had come all that way especially to buy the mirror. He came to me and started bidding me for it. His final offer was £1,750.

He left his address and telephone number, just in case His Grace might be interested."

"Not a hope. I'm sure the answer would be a very firm 'no'." After a few more minutes' chat with Dick, I joined Terence Coffey in the lounge. He was comfortably ensconced in a large armchair, sipping a cognac. I told him about the mirror and that I was relieved that everything had gone according to plan. Terence shrugged.

"So? The chances are that it'll finish up in store at Eaton with dozens of others. You know, we lesser serfs, who don't move in the ducal circle, but do our bit looking after the 'privy purse' might, thanks to His Grace's tax liability, have to make him £34,400 just to indulge his little whim to own a mirror he obviously doesn't need."

When I stopped to think about it, there was a lot of truth in what Coffey said. Had I kept my mouth shut, as we passed Carton, I could have saved myself quite a lot of bother. Little did I know what was to come!

The following evening, when I returned to Dublin, there was a message for me to telephone Dick immediately, most urgent. I did as requested. Dick had gone to Carton with the van from the removal firm, which had been booked in advance by me, to take the mirror to Fort William.

When they got there the auctioneer's clerk would not let them take it, in spite of the fact that Dick had paid for it the evening before and had the receipted account. Lord Brocket claimed that it was a fixture and was, literally, built into the wall. In his opinion the vendors, the Duke of Leinster and the Mallaby-Deeley Trustees, had no right to offer it for sale. It turned out that it was a well-known piece by no lesser personage than Thomas Chippendale.

Dick, wisely, had not waited for my return and had phoned George McVeagh. The latter having first contacted the auctioneers, phoned Ridley. It seemed to McVeagh that Brocket was right, lot 608 was a fixture. I had only just put the phone down, after talking to Dick, when George Ridley came on the line. He'd just seen the Duke. He was seething. He'd bought and paid for the mirror and he was going to have it. Amongst other things he had suggested I should take some men, break into Carton and, if necessary, remove it by force. I started to object strongly, but Ridley told me to calm down and forget it. He was just telling me what His Grace had said so that I would appreciate how seriously he was taking the matter. Eventually George ended his call. I went into my room and poured myself a large whiskey – I needed it. There was no doubt, at times, my employer acted like a very spoilt small child – I want so I must have!

The ruckus continued, unabated, throughout the following weeks. The Duke shouting 'I want it', a baron retorting 'you can't have it' and a further duke (Leinster) claiming 'it's mine to sell or do what I want with'. The auctioneer, Mr Townsend, was suffering from a nervous breakdown! McVeagh had taken counsel's opinion. It wasn't very encouraging, but in spite of this he was going ahead in accordance with Westminster's instructions and preparing to issue a writ. A lawsuit, which at one stage seemed inevitable, would publicise two dukes and a baron fighting over a mirror!

I had been back to look – twice. Once on my own and once with a very experienced auctioneer and valuer. The latter was adamant that the mirror was a fixture. Ridley, too, agreed that it should never have been offered for sale. Now all he had to do was to persuade the Duke that it had all been a mistake, but this wasn't easy. Hugh Richard Arthur was like a terrier with a rat – he wouldn't let go. My sympathy was with Ronnie Brocket, a charming man who I knew and was to come to know much better in the future.

Notwithstanding the 'Carton mirror' saga, life went on. May saw the first appearance of exhibits from the Duke's Shorthorn herd at the Royal Dublin Society's Spring Show. The results were spectacular, the Duke's entries were sweeping the board in the Shorthorn section. From telegrams received, the Duke appeared to be delighted, but I very much doubted if there was any genuine interest in the achievements of his cattle. After all he'd never bothered to look at them, even when he had visited the farm! It was ironic that the cow, Holmescales Annetta, which took the supreme honours had not been bred by the Duke. She was one of the three that I had purchased at the Shorthorn Sales at Penrith prior to the first shipment going into quarantine. I didn't think anything we were being 'given' from Eaton was good enough to take the top awards in the showring!

Sad to say the Duke, probably the largest landowner in Great Britain, was no farmer. He was no modern-day 'Coke of Holkham'. Thomas William Coke, Earl of Leicester, was undoubtedly the greatest pioneer of agricultural improvements this country has ever known. He revolutionized farming at the end of the eighteenth and the beginning of the nineteenth century. Nevertheless, the Duke, quite properly, received the kudos for the successes his employees achieved with his herds and in estate management.

It was not long after the Spring Show that I was notified that the Duke and Duchess were to visit Ireland. I was to meet them at 1.15pm at the Shelbourne, I was there at 12.30pm. One didn't keep His Grace waiting, at least not if one worked for him. As I entered the hotel, I checked with the hall porter. No, His Grace had not come in yet. He and the Duchess had gone out about twenty minutes ago. I walked on into the lounge. Slightly to my right I heard a voice.

"Hullo Twist. Come and join me for drink." I turned, it was Lord Brocket. "What'll you have?" I explained I was meeting the Duke and Duchess for lunch at 1.15pm.

"Fine, you've loads of time." I sipped dry sherry as I chatted with his lordship. He never once mentioned the mirror. He mostly told me of his plans for Carton and what he proposed doing on the farm. He was excellent company and the time went quickly. Just before 1.00pm I must have been subconsciously glancing at my wristwatch, for Brocket laughed and stood up.

"Don't worry. I won't let you be seen hobnobbing with the enemy! I'll go and hide in a corner. Bend Or hasn't a hope of winning. I know he usually gets his own way, but not this time. When I move into Carton, you must come and have dinner with me." With that he crossed to the far corner of the lounge and seated himself with his back to the entrance. I had only just settled back in my chair when the Duke appeared, stopping in the entrance as he looked round the lounge. He was early, it had been a near thing and as I stood up he saw me.

"Ah! There you are Twist." His voice boomed across the room. He was not noted for whispering! "Glad you're early. Heard anything from that bloody brewer about my mirror?" I felt as though I'd like a hole to open in the floor and swallow me up! At least that was until I heard a very distinct chuckle coming from a large armchair with its back to the entrance!

Five minutes later the Duchess joined us and we went in to lunch. Having got the mirror out of his system, at least for the present, His Grace was in excellent form. He was anxious to know how things were progressing regarding buying another property at Maynooth. I told him that McVeagh expected to complete the next day. Six weeks previously I had heard that a large property of some 480 acres, adjoining Donaghstown, was on the market. The asking price was £50,000, just over £100 per acre – a ridiculously high figure.

I discussed the possible purchase with George Ridley. He wasn't happy. He felt it could lead to problems with the government's Land Commission. They had considerable power and were able to acquire land with comparative ease. When they did this they divided big tracts into holdings of some twenty-five to thirty acres. Whilst this provided homes for migrants from the more rugged areas in the west of Ireland, it was tantamount to developing a peasant community and a low standard of agricultural husbandry. George was concerned that they might think the Duke was buying too much land. However, both McVeagh and I felt sure that to buy this farm must be right. Eventually, we persuaded Ridley to mention it to the Duke. Rather to the former's surprise, 'The Owner' thought it was an excellent idea. I was to go ahead and arrange the purchase in the Duchess's name. This decision was followed by the usual wrangling over the price, traditionally part of any deal in Ireland, eventually it was agreed at £23,000!

Ridley had, to a degree, been right in his fears. On 23 June there was a heated debate in Dáil Eireann, the Irish Parliament, about non-nationals buying up land. One TD (Irish MP) became very excited, claiming that the Duke of Westminster, a Sassenach, had recently bought a large farm in Co. Kildare. He was quickly corrected by another member of the House, who pointed out that it was the Duchess who had purchased it and that she was as Irish as the last speaker.

It was around this time I learned that my most excellent 'digs' at Dartmouth Road were unlikely to continue as the house was to be turned into flats. Bryanstown, the property that we were in the throes of purchasing at Maynooth, had a large house which had been neglected but was structurally sound. The drawing room and the adjoining dining room had been knocked into one and they were being used as a machinery shed, while concrete steps had been built up the outside and the two major bedrooms were being used as an oat loft. The remainder of the house was divided to accommodate two farm workers and their families. One of these was the foreman and he was moving to the vendor's property in Co. Meath. There was an empty cottage on Donaghstown, this could house the other family. I had my eye on Bryanstown. It would make a beautiful home. The thing was, could I persuade Ridley to carry out the required renovation? It would greatly add to the value of the property as a whole.

The Duke seemed most interested and said he thought we

might all go and look at it after lunch. Nothing would have given me greater pleasure. Possibly His Grace might be persuaded to call at Derrinstown too and see his cow that took supreme honours at the Spring Show. Just then I was called to the phone. It was McVeagh to say he'd completed the purchase of Bryanstown, a day earlier than expected. Whilst at the phone I made a quick call to Dick Powley to let know that the Duke was talking about visiting the farms. When I got back to the table the Duke seemed very pleased to learn that the purchase had been completed. He asked about the house. I told him about its current state, but that it could easily be restored and would make a lovely home. Suddenly he asked where I lived. I told him adding that, alas, it would not be for much longer as the house was being turned in to flats. He was silent for a moment.

"Hmm, well you better have this place you've just bought for me done up and live in it. No need to buy any furniture, there's any amount at Eaton. I'll tell Bryant to send over what you need when the time comes. If you're occupying the house there can't be any chat about absentee landlords." Then he laughed – a real chuckle. "Better be careful though. We don't want you shot, Twist. Land agents were highly prized trophies during the Troubles – no closed season for shooting them!" His Grace seemed highly amused, still laughing he added. "Talk to Ridley about it. Come on Nance, we won't bother to go to Maynooth after all. It might make us late getting to the Fort. We'll have a look, Twist, the next time we're over." With that he rose from the table and within minutes they were gone.

Some weeks later I received a copy of a letter, dated 8 July 1949, from Lord Brockett to the Duke on the subject of the mirror. It was most gracious, acknowledging that no doubt the Duke was most disappointed, but the mirror really was a fixture and should never have been included in the auction. The Duke totally ignored it. On 26 July George Ridley wrote a most diplomatic letter to Bend Or, strongly advising that he should answer Brocket's letter. Further that he, the Duke, really had no hope of a lawsuit going his way. So ended, what to me, was a thoroughly churlish and somewhat degrading incident.

Whilst all this had been going on, George Ridley had quietly been consolidating his position as Chief Agent, as well as becoming firmly entrenched as a trustee and executor of the Duke's will. It had been the Duke himself who had formed the Trust as a young man in 1901.

Over the years 'The Owner', rightly or wrongly, had come to the conclusion that his trustees were working against him, rather than for him. With this in mind he consulted Basil Kerr, his great friend and confidant. The outcome was that George Ridley was appointed as a trustee. The Duke wanted a man on the inside, someone in whom he had complete faith and whom he could be sure would always work for his interests. He could have found no more loyal or fervent supporter than Ridley. However, the appointment was no sinecure. It may have more than exceeded the wildest dreams of the rather sickly boy who went to work in the Duke's forestry department at Eaton in 1926, but His Grace had given Ridley 'a hard row to hoe'. Tradition was well established in the London office, at 53 Davies Street. A standard of management had been developed, over a period of more than three centuries which had changed to a remarkably small degree.

The estate was administered, most properly, by the Duke's lawyers, Boodle Hatfield & Co., but it has to be said, with no great thought for the future. The senior partners of the firm acted as agents. There was one surveyor employed by the Duke and one architect, but no management team working exclusively for him. In fact a quite extraordinary situation existed whereby the majority of the leases were negotiated by independent agents. This was one thing, George told me, he intended to change immediately. However, this was far from being a popular move. There were too many people who, whilst being completely honest were, to use a modern slang idiom, 'on a very nice little earner.'

Whilst very much part of the inner sanctum working with the Chief Agent, I was not directly involved with the London estate, but was still very aware as to what was happening. I often thought that George used me as a 'sounding board', for we would have long telephone conversations several evenings a week. To the extent that, when I moved to Bryanstown, old Mrs Caulfield, who had the Post Office and so, automatically, the telephone exchange at Maynooth, would frequently ring me around 6.00pm to know if I intended calling Mr Ridley during the course of the evening, because, if I did, would I please refrain from doing so between 7.00pm and 7.45pm, or whatever the time might have been, as there was a programme on the wireless which she particularly wished to hear.

To call George at his home at Eccleston was not, in those days, just a simple matter of dialling the number. I had to ring Maynooth; Mrs Caulfield then passed the call on to Dublin. They had to get through to Liverpool, who in turn transferred the call on to Chester where, with luck, they made the final connection to Eccleston. Quite a performance! Any one section of the link could be engaged, often causing long delays.

The year quickly passed. I was comfortably settled in Bryanstown, adequately furnished from Eaton, and a married couple, the McManuses had been supplied by the estate to look after my needs. I was almost developing routine! The only thing that was a constant irritant was 'the almighty dollar'. It seemed that the Duke could never have enough. I was everlastingly being instructed to go and see Ikey Bell and say 'more, more, more'. The poor man kept telling me that, whilst he was delighted to help his dear friend in every way he could, he did not wish to transfer from America more money than he required for his personal use. He was delighted to let Bend Or have such dollars as he required for this purpose, providing, of course, he received their equivalent in sterling, but he really *didn't* want to bring over more than he needed personally. It seemed that the Duke was quite incapable of grasping this.

Nineteen forty-nine saw further expansion into agricultural estates and forestry in England. Part of the Melton Constable Estate in Norfolk was purchased, to be followed later in the year by the acquisition of Manby from the Earl of Yarborough, part of his Brockelsby Estate. Late in the year the Coddington Estate in Cheshire was added to the rapidly growing acreage. Such purchases dwarfed anything that happened in Ireland, but the ultimate goal was the same.

The autumn once more saw the name Westminster to the fore in estate development. George Ridley put forward a plan for all the farms on the Eaton Estate, some fifty-two of them, to become attested. This meant all the cattle being free of tuberculosis and subject to regular checks by Ministry-approved vets. It also meant the modernization of the buildings and this was the real attraction. It enabled further money to be put where it was subject to a lower rate of death duties!

The proposed upgrading of both the herds and buildings received a great deal of publicity in both the agricultural and daily press. Much of the work on the byres could be put through the books as general maintenance work which was the liability of the landlord, namely the Duke, and was recoverable at nineteen shillings and sixpence in the pound. However, much was straightforward capital expenditure, the Duke, or more accurately the trustees, finding £150,000 for this purpose. Little was done from a purely altruistic viewpoint, which was perfectly reasonable under the prevailing circumstances. Rents were to be increased according to the amount of capital invested in each farm. However, George Ridley was not terribly happy, in so far that the Duke would not allow him to increase the rent by five per cent on the money involved; which, incidentally was the maximum that could be charged by law for such development. The Duke was no farmer and had no apparent interest in agriculture; he did, however, have a very high regard for his tenants, most of whom he had known well since he was a boy. He gave instructions that only two per cent interest was to be charged, two per cent at the most. Once again the Duke showed how magnanimous he could be, particularly when it affected the tenants on the Eaton Estate or the workers.

One of the first problems Ridley had to face, when taking over at Eaton, was that a large number of tied cottages where the accommodation went with the job were occupied by retired couples, widows and widowers. George told the Duke that he really would have to evict them. The cottages were urgently wanted for farm and estate staff. George told me he had received a 'right rocket' from the Duke for even making such a suggestion. There was a potential building site at Handbridge on the outskirts of Chester owned by the Duke. He gave instructions that this was to be developed.

Twenty-four houses and sixteen flats were built and the occupants of the tied cottages, so urgently required on the estate, were moved into these, some paying as little as three shillings (15p) a week rent! Whilst the farm buildings on the estate were being modernized, so were some three hundred cottages. The aim was to make them comparable with any town accommodation in the way of amenities and this included a bathroom in every cottage, something absent from many country cottages even in the late 40s. This work was done at a cost of some £45,000, around £2 million at today's rates.

Life was never dull! It seemed as though I could not get on with my job, agriculture and estate management, without some diversion. The latter appeared in one instance in the form of a Finnish refugee ship. An ancient 580-ton motor ship had arrived in Cork, bearing 385 displaced persons. The 'passengers' were made up of Finns, Estonians, Lithuanians,

Latvians, Poles, Yugo-Slavs, Czechs, one Swede and one Hungarian. I had read of their arrival in the daily papers, had felt momentary compassion for them and then given the matter little further thought. It was, therefore, something of a surprise when I received a phone call from the Lord Mayor of Cork, Mr S McCarthy. He wished to read me a telegram he had received. It was as follows:

> 'Would like to assist emigrants in ship *Victory* lying in Cork. Will donate £250 to assist passage in another ship or to use as you suggest. Please wire any suggestions. Westminster.'

Two hundred and fifty pounds does not sound a lot, but it was roughly equivalent to £10,000 now. It was so typical of the Duke's generosity to those in genuine need. The Lord Mayor was delighted, but had no idea where to send his reply. He had telephoned Fort William. He'd been told that the Duke was not in residence and it was suggested by John Lynch, the resident butler, that he should contact me. I could not tell him where the Duke was as he moved around with a restless regularity which was hard to keep up with! However, I assured His Worship the Mayor that I would quickly locate His Grace and ring him back as soon as I had done so. I telephoned Bill Bryan.

"Ah! You've saved me a call. I was just going to ring you. 'The Owner' wants me to cross to Ireland tonight. You are to meet me and we are to go to Cork immediately. You are to contact the Mayor and make an appointment for us to see him tomorrow, so that we can discuss the matter of the refugees with him. His Grace is most concerned about them."

He had good reason to be worried, for conditions on the ship were, to say the least, very grim. It was a terrible leaky old 'tub', barely seaworthy. I learned, when I phoned the Mayor, that the unfortunate occupants were being temporarily housed in a disused military camp at Rockgrove, whilst the condition of the ship was being assessed by the authorities.

Bill and I reached Cork soon after noon on 4 October. We were warmly greeted by Mr McCarthy and a long discussion took place with him and his advisers. In due course we made our way down to the docks, boarded the *Victory* and met her skipper – Captain Ernst. Bill, as an ex-naval Lieutenant Commander, was I felt the one to pass comment in this sphere, but one wouldn't have had to be very knowledgeable on maritime matters to realise that the *Victory* was a load of junk! As we toured the rust-covered hulk Bill's reaction was one of disbelief. That the *Victory* had crossed the North Sea, rounded Land's End and made her way to Ireland on her mercy voyage was, he felt, nothing short of miraculous.

We then visited Rockgrove, where we met and talked to a number of the refugees. They had been told of the Duke's help and were pathetically grateful. It was difficult to converse with them, for none had any more than a few words of English, but, by degrees, we learned that the majority wanted to go to Canada. At last, having had our hands shaken to the extent of being positively embarrassing we left the camp, promising to do all we could to help. We returned to the Mayor's parlour. It was by then after five o'clock. He offered us tea, or would we sooner have 'a drop of the hard stuff'? We opted for the latter.

The Mayor produced a bottle of 'Paddy' from his desk drawer – the local whiskey produced by Cork Distillery. While we gratefully sipped our drinks, Bill and I formulated a message for the Duke. We decided to phone Eaton Hall. I put the call through. I didn't, for one minute, expect to speak to His Grace, it would be a case of giving a message to Richard Chapman, or whoever was on duty. It turned out to be Richard. I hung on whilst he conveyed our report to 'The Owner'. It seemed an interminable time before Richard came back on the line. I was to immediately give the Mayor a cheque for a further £250. In addition we were to make certain that alternative berths were found for the refugees to continue their journey to Canada, or wherever they wished to go. This the Lord Mayor assured us would be done. Further, that he would be in close touch with me, so that I could keep the Duke informed as to what was happening.

Feeling totally drained, Bill and I at last left for Fort William, where we were spending the night. We had only just entered the house when I heard the phone ring. John Lynch who had been about to show us up to our rooms, departed to answer it. He came back within a few minutes, Mr McCarthy wished to speak to me. He sounded in a most jubilant mood and I wondered if the 'Paddy' might have received a little hardship after we had left! The reason for his call was to say that he felt sure I would like to know that one of the Polish refugees, Mrs Felicjo Laanisite, had just given birth to twins in Cork hospital. She wanted to know if the Duke would mind if she named them after him. I replied that I thought he would be honoured and, as requested, gave the Mayor the Duke's Christian names. Adding, as an afterthought, that to his friends he was know as Bend Or or Benny. I have often wondered if, somewhere in the world, there is a Pole with the somewhat unique name of Bend Or Laanisite.

7
The Absurdities of the Rich

It was somewhere around the beginning of 1950 that the pseudonym of 'The Owner' for the Duke was replaced by 'The Chief'. As Terence Coffey remarked to me one day, he was never quite sure whether he was supposed to be playing 'Red Indians' or had joined the Boy Scouts! Whichever it was the real chief was without doubt George Ridley. He worked tirelessly to achieve his goal, often to the detriment of his health. However, he was not alone in this. Several of us suffered, carried along by George's enthusiasm, but to a lesser degree. I started developing the most agonising boils and having partial blackouts and dizzy turns. I went to see a doctor; he assured me it was nothing that a good holiday would not put right. I was he said, suffering from being over tired and stressed. My immediate reaction was that I could not possibly take a holiday and made an appointment to have a second opinion.

The diagnosis was the same. However, this second medic was adamant that I took a holiday, immediately. It was imperative that I did so unless I wanted to seriously damage my health. Further, that if I didn't do what he said he'd contact the Duke and tell him what an inconsiderate employer he was. I was horrified and immediately capitulated, for the doctor in question had a great reputation for being a man of his word. Anyway, I'd not had a holiday since I started to work for His Grace, I was certainly due one.

I returned to my office and tried to contact Ridley, only to learn that he was in bed and very far from well. I asked his wife, Mary, to tell him I just had to have a break, but would keep in touch with the Dublin office. I arranged with Honor Reveille to contact me if anything really urgent happened. In this category I included even a whisper that His Grace might be coming to Ireland. With that I departed to the west of Ireland to relax and fish for trout, which in those days were plentiful. As I drove across Ireland I began to unwind. Before leaving Dublin the last thing I'd done was to phone Bill Bryan. He was of the opinion that it was most unlikely that Their Graces would be coming to Ireland in the immediate future. He had just returned from Mimizan, where 'The Chief' was enjoying the glorious spring weather and, Bill felt, was momentarily settled. But then one never knew with His Grace!

I had been at Oughterard, on the edge of Lough Corrib, for six days and was feeling much much better. I was relaxed and starting to think about work. The boils had gone and I hadn't had a dizzy turn for three days. Another week and I'd be ready to take on anything. It was around 7.00pm, when I was having a pre-dinner drink with other anglers, all of us telling of the one that got away, when I was called to the phone. It was Honor Reveille. The Duke and Duchess were crossing to Ireland that night! There was message that the Duke might want to see me in the morning. Cursing volubly I packed, had a hasty dinner and set off on the four-and-a-half to five-hour journey back to Bryanstown. So much for my planned two weeks of peace and quiet, the minimum the doctor said I should take.

I was in the office the following morning before Mrs Reveille, ready to go round to the Shelbourne if summoned. As I waited I set to work to clear my desk, it was quite amazing what had accumulated in a week. At 10.30am I asked Mrs Reveille to phone the Shelbourne and have a word with Miss McCarthy, the head receptionist to try to find out if the latter had any ideas about the Duke's movements. She had. He was just leaving for Lismore! Inwardly I cursed, I'd rushed back for nothing. I looked out of the window; it was a perfect day for fishing. Momentarily I thought of heading back for Oughterard, but knew this was wishful thinking. Whilst the Duke was in Ireland I had to be on standby. I cleared up everything requiring my attention at the office and headed back to Bryanstown for lunch.

I had just started my dinner, that evening, when the telephone rang. It was Richard Chapman. His Grace would like me to be at Fort William by 11.00am the following morning. I enquired if His Grace wished me to stay the night? Richard replied that he didn't think so. I put down the phone. I could have wept – why the hell hadn't he sent for me when he was in Dublin? To be sure of being at the Fort on time, I'd have to leave Maynooth around 6.00am! I was beginning to wish I hadn't been quite so hasty in turning down an offer some time back from Lord Brocket to go to him as agent at Carton. I had been very tempted, but his Lordship was noted for going through land agents with amazing regularity, it was better to stay where I was. After all hadn't Ridley clearly said that we were working for our future, as well as to save the Grosvenor millions from the clutches of the taxman?

I had an excellent run down to Lismore. I was in such good time that I called in at the farm to see if Lawlor, the steward, was there. He was, deep in conversation with the owner/driver of a bulldozer, which had just arrived. There was one final land reclamation project to be completed. Quite a small job, some two to three acres of scrub with a stream running through it, to be cleared, cultivated and seeded down to grass. It was part of a small farm that abounded Fort William and which had been purchased about two years before. It lay between the farmyard and the River Blackwater. When this was done there would be no wasteland left on the estate – a fact that Ben Lawlor was inordinately proud of.

I gathered that operations would commence immediately after lunch. The 'dozer' driver hoped to have his part finished by the following evening. I made a mental note to take a look at what progress had been made before I headed for home later in the day. I looked at my wristwatch, it was 10.50am, time I drove on down to the house. It was 11.35am before the Duke appeared! He greeted me warmly and told me had made a wonderful discovery. I wondered what was coming. It transpired he'd found some wild orchids. I don't think I ever saw him so excited over anything. It is of course the little things in life that can give the most pleasure to those who have everything.

"Looked them up in a book last night, Twist. Pretty sure they're the Early Purple Orchid. There's a lot of them. Lovely! According to the book, if that is the one, it was known to the early Greeks and for centuries in this country it has been considered an ingredient for a love potion." He laughed loudly. "Expect that accounts for the maids having babies." Each winter it seemed at least one of the maids at the Fort became pregnant. The Duke used to refer to it as 'the winter games.'

"Come on, I'll show you where these orchids are. Just wait until I see if Nancy wants to come." Off he went in search of the Duchess, leaving me cogitating in the hall on two things. Firstly, it was a hell of a long way to come to look at wild orchids. Secondly, it was the first time he'd ever referred to the Duchess, to me, by her christian name – I rather think it was the last. He was back in a few minutes.

"No, she's busy. Come on dogs."

Dringalo gave him a baleful look and trotted off to the library. His companion, many years younger, leapt around, barking with excitement. The Duke selected a hat from selection of eight or ten that graced a table in the hall. It seemed that he kept a supply at each residence, mostly trilbies of a variety of shapes and colours. I remember once all hell was let loose when the Duke arrived at Fort William and found John Lynch had had all his hats cleaned and reblocked. It seemed the more greasy and battered they were the more the Duke liked them!

We set off briskly up the drive, the dachshund

scampering along, barking in front. We turned off into a field after we had gone a short distance. There was no doubt the Duke was in excellent form. He looked really happy as he strode out across the rich green grass, clouds of smoke drifting away as he puffed contentedly on a large cigar. Suddenly he stopped and gazed out across the river to the far side of the valley. The whole area was a mass of scrub woodland. Waving vaguely in the general direction, he said.

"Think we should buy that, Twist. Suppose the regulations governing reafforestation are much the same here as in England?"

I replied that they were, but I doubted he would be able to buy the area in question, as it belonged to the Duke of Devonshire.

Bend Or gave a snort.

"Well he ought to look after his woodland better. The chap can afford it."

We were now walking down in to a shallow valley. It suddenly dawned on me that we were heading straight for the area about to be reclaimed! The Duke paused on the edge of the wasteland.

"There's a path here somewhere. Ah, here it is." He pushed passed an elder bush, I followed. We were on a track worn by cattle, over many years, going down to drink from the stream.

"There they are – see?" it wasn't the case of just one or two orchids, there were dozens of them. I moved on down the well-worn path. I'm no botanist, but it seemed to me that there were two varieties. I drew the Duke's attention to this, he was delighted.

"Lovely! Look here, Twist. Have this area fenced – properly. Make sure no livestock or rabbits can get in. Have the briars cleared, some paths made and put a footbridge across the stream, make a wild garden of it. Come on, let's get back to the house and have a drink."

I looked at my watch. In less than half an hour the

bulldozer was due to start crashing through the future orchid sanctuary! I had to see Lawlor and quickly.

"Will you excuse me for ten minutes Your Grace? I must see Lawlor before he goes out after his lunch." The farm men stopped from noon until 1.00pm for their midday meal. The Duke told me not to be long and walked off towards the house. I almost ran to the farm. I hastily told Lawlor what had to be done and that no way was the bulldozer to start work. His face was a study.

"But them's only weeds. Get that scrub cleared, seeded down with good grass, a touch of fertiliser and we can carry another six or seven bullocks."

In spite of his obvious displeasure at such poor husbandry, the answer remained the same. Further, I told him not only should the orchids be made safe behind a rabbit and stock-proof fence, but that he'd better gas any rabbit burrows within the enclosure. He, poor man, was left speechless by the absurdities of the rich! It took six men three weeks to develop the orchid 'arbour'.

Whether the Duke ever went near it again I never knew, he certainly never mentioned it. I, on the other hand, inspected it about once a month to ensure that all was well. At around 3.15pm I set off back to Bryanstown. The last thing the Duke said to me was "See what you can find out about that land across the river. I'd rather like to buy it." As I drove the twisting road across to Cahir I thought, who ever said that pace of life in Ireland was slow had never had dealings with the 2nd Duke of Westminster!

A visit from George Ridley was always revitalising, not only because he certainly kept one on one's toes, but he was also excellent company and had a fund of ducal anecdotes. It was in the autumn of 1950 that he came to Ireland for three days. A really long visit!

The first night he stayed with me at Bryanstown. I had previously asked him if he'd like me to arrange a small dinner party, or would he sooner have a quiet evening? He opted for the latter. After an excellent meal prepared by my housekeeper, Mrs McManus, we adjourned to the drawing room. George was relaxed and in a mood to reminisce. Had he ever told me about Detmar Blow? He hadn't.

It appeared that Detmar Blow was an architect who had done work for the Duke on the London Estate. The latter took such a liking to Blow that he offered him the job as his private secretary. Detmar, history has it, jumped at the opportunity. It seems from the outset that Blow had set out to cheat his friend and employer. He was a man of considerable charm and the Duke put his full trust in him. Amongst other things the Duke empowered his secretary to sign on all his accounts, including the personal one out of which a considerable sum was paid, quarterly, to ex-wives and other ladies who, from time to time, had graced the ducal bed! However, nothing the Duke could do or say would persuade Blow to sign cheques on this account. He claimed that they were of far too personal a nature for him, a mere secretary, to deal with. A compromise was agreed. Blow would write out the cheques and dispatch them, but the Duke must sign them.

This seemed to work admirably for quite a while. Detmar would wait until the Duke was about to rush off somewhere, he would then insist that Bend Or sign the cheques before he left. This invariably led to the secretary hastily turning the corners of the cheques, still in the book and exposing just enough of each one for the Duke to sign. The latter, it seems, never looked at what he was signing.

One day, when the Duke was about to leave Bourdon House for the station on his way to France, Blow rushed in to say that Bend Or must sign the quarterly cheques before he left. The latter was furious and only agreed to do so if his secretary came to the station with him. He'd sign the wretched things en route. Detmar balanced an attaché case on his knee to rest the chequebook on, whilst the Duke leaned across and signed as the corners were turned over. They had nearly finished when another car drove into them. Both the Duke and Detmar Blow landed on the floor. As he picked himself and the chequebook up, the Duke saw he'd just signed a cheque, for a very considerable sum, made payable to his secretary. He said nothing.

No great damage had been done to the car and Duke instructed his chauffeur to continue, as fast as he could, to Victoria Station. He was anxious to get to his beloved Mimizan. (It was somewhat ironic that the Château Woolsack had been designed by Blow!)

The Duke spent several days there before he sent for the senior partner of his London accountants. The Duke's instructions were explicit – investigate the account in question and see if any other cheques had been drawn in favour of Detmar Blow. The accountant returned to London and quickly reported that he had gone back to the beginning of the current year. His findings were quite staggering. He had discovered a number of cheques, amounting to many thousands of pounds, made payable to Detmar Blow, all signed by the Duke. The latter told the accountant to delve no further. He was deeply distressed that anyone to whom he had given his friendship should have so blatantly deceived him. Bend Or wrote to his secretary dismissing him and giving him one week in which to leave the country. Further, he said that he had no intention of taking legal action – he did not prosecute his friends, nor was he going to seek reparation. The Duke's dislike for publicity and his sense of loyalty to his friends undoubtedly saved Blow from a long and severe jail sentence. George was a good raconteur. I filled up his empty glass.

"That's quite incredible. It certainly was a case of 'crime pays'. Do you know how much he got away with?"

George sipped his drink.

"I've no idea. He'd been defrauding the Duke for years. But you haven't heard the best bit. Blow returned to England after a few years, bought a large country estate, I believe in Shropshire, built up a first-class pheasant shoot and then had the gall to write asking the Duke to come and shoot with him. How's that for pure bloody arrogance and cheek?"

"Did 'The Chief' go?"

"No! But neither did he make Blow leave the country again. I'm sure, over the years, there have been many minor fiddles, but nothing to compare with Detmar's grand scale. There was a factor in Scotland, whom the Duke thought the world of, they were great friends. Anyway this chap proved to be an ingenious rogue and looked after himself at 'The Chief's' expense for a number years."

George went on to relate how this factor had a clause in his agreement that allowed him to run a limited number of ewes on the estate. I think he said fifty. Mountain flocks rarely average more than one lamb reared per ewe by the time they have overcome the hazards of the weather and such predators as foxes. To the latter, on the Reay Forest Estates could be added golden eagles, beautiful to see, but no friend of the shepherds! However, in spite of all these obstacles the factor managed to sell around two hundred lambs every year at the Lairg autumn sale, ostensibly the progeny of his fifty ewes! It transpired he'd been creaming off the pick of the Duke's lambs for years.

Ridley went on to say that this wasn't the only little racket this 'friend' of the Duke's had been running. Quite simply, he still kept employees who had died on the wages sheet. Each week he drew their pay, even stamped their insurance card. By doing the latter he completely hoodwinked the accountants when they came to do the annual audit. It had been a most lucrative deception. I do not remember how long George said this had been going on, but certainly many years. When the fraud was eventually uncovered, The Duke could not believe that anyone whom he looked upon as a trusted friend could have behaved in such an underhand way. As in the case of Detmar Blow no legal action was taken, nor was repayment of the stolen money asked for. The culprit was given seven days in which to leave the country and told never to come back.

Apart from George's visit being a Commanding Officer's inspection of the Irish properties, he had another mission to fulfil, 'The Chief' had heard that Ikey Bell was in the throes of buying a substantial farm in Co. Meath, for his daughter Di and her husband Colonel Willie Newell. The cost for those days was high. Bend Or obviously saw it as a dollar opportunity and had sent his chief agent to ask Ikey not to do anything until they'd had a talk. George was not happy, but, as he said, he could not meddle in the Duke's personal affairs, on this occasion he was just the messenger boy.

Whilst these lesser machinations were going on, great strides were being made in acquiring further agricultural properties. The Pale Estates had been purchased in Wales, and in Scotland, Gobernuisgach had been added to the Reay Forest Estates. However, land was not the only thing that had been added to the Duke's Scottish interests. A fishing and transport business was purchased at Kinlochbervie. This in turn was to lead to the purchase of a wholesale fish company in Aberdeen. The latter when required, could be used as depot or for selling catches for which inadequate bids had been made at Kinlochbervie.

One thing led to another and it was not long before the Duke, his enterprises booming, was almost forced into buying the Sutherland Transport and Trading Company. The transaction had the blessing of the government, in spite of the fact that its objective was the complete nationalization of all public transport! The Duke's new acquisition meant that he had the responsibility of running virtually all the bus services within the county, plus the ambulance service and the delivery of the mail. This venture received quite a lot of publicity. One 'wag' in Dublin asked me if it was true that the Duchess was a 'clippy' on the Lairg – Lochmore bus? I replied that I hadn't heard anything to that effect, but felt quite certain that, if it would further the Duke's cause, she would do it without a moment's hesitation.

The 'cause' seemed to flourish. The fishing enterprise was expanding to a degree that fishermen, together with their boats, were coming to settle in Kinlochbervie from as far away as Lossiemouth. It seemed that there had never been such prosperity in that remote northern area. The Duke may have had no great interest in his Dairy Shorthorns, but he certainly took a most lively interest in what was happening in his beloved Sutherlandshire. However, not even the Duke's money, nor his staff's enthusiasm and expertise could establish a viable cattle venture on the mountains surrounding Lochmore. Whilst it was found that several breeds could withstand the penetrating cold experienced during the winter on the Reay Forest Estates, rain proved to be the insurmountable barrier. With a normal annual rainfall well in excess of one hundred inches, the cattle were virtually never dry and, consequently, did not thrive. Many years later, whilst managing an estate in the heart of the Wicklow mountains in Ireland, 'The Owner' insisted on trying a similar scheme. It proved as disastrous. Rain again being the cause for its failure.

'Operation Death Duties' advanced within the British Isles at a quite phenomenal rate, but Ridley was still desperate to get money out of the country and into the real estate overseas. With this in mind application was made through the courts to be allowed to invest money in East Africa and Canada. George's 'dream' was setting out along a road leading to reality.

8
A Working Wedding Morning

Yet another estate, Park Hatch in Surrey, was added to the Duke's ever-increasing acreage in 1951. This brought the total purchases up to around 100,000 acres, at a cost of some £2 million. On this sum thirty-six per cent death duties would be saved when the time came. All very satisfactory, but there was still much to be done. As estates were acquired, work began on repairs as quickly as it was feasible to do so. Repairs ranked, for tax relief, at nineteen shillings and sixpence in the pound, whilst improvements provided relief over a period of ten years.

During the time George Ridley had been in office some £720,000 had already been spent on the maintenance of agricultural properties and one must assume that this had added at least this amount to their value, thus storing up wealth for future generations of Grosvenors. The beauty of this ploy was that it had only cost the Duke £18,000 in real money. A recent court decision referred to as the Northumberland Case, the outcome of which was to release both personal and trust money for immediate use, suggested that it might well cost Bend Or nothing. Thanks to the findings of the court it seemed he could get a refund on the money he spent from his trustees.

I had been following up the Duke's instructions with regard to purchasing the land across the river from Fort William, but without success. It was mid-March when I was summoned to Lismore. 'The Chief' wanted to know what progress I had made. I had to reply 'none'. I explained that Captain FitzGerald, known to everyone as Fitz, while keen to help, was first and foremost agent to the Devonshires. He had been unable to obtain a decision from *his* duke, mine was very obviously not pleased at this news.

It was a spring-like day. The Duke decided we should go outside and, looking as black as thunder, he stalked out onto the drive. There was a local meet of the foxhounds, and the Duchess, who had been a keen follower of the hounds for many years, was going. Just as we were walking across the big sweep of the drive in front of the house the Duchess came into sight, astride a bay gelding. Nancy was an excellent horsewoman and sat a horse as though she was moulded to it.

She was followed by one of the grooms on another of her hunters. She called out cheerfully.

"We've plenty of time, so I thought I'd come round this way to say cheerio. I won't stay out too late." The Duke scowled.

"Ah, well, think we'll go back to Eaton tonight." That meant that they would have to leave by the middle of the afternoon. So much for the Duchess's day hunting! Without a second's hesitation she jumped off her horse, passed the reins to the groom and told him to take the horses back to the stable. Smiling, she linked her arm through the Duke's and led him towards the house.

"Of course Benny, whatever you say."

She showed no disappointment, or animosity. It was, I thought, both one of the most unselfish and at the same time most selfish acts I had ever witnessed. Frankly, I thought the Duchess behaved like a saint! Whether Bend Or was suffering from a moment of pique because at his age he could no longer hunt, or whether he was taking out his annoyance on his wife because he hadn't had his way regarding the land across the river, I'll never know, but I rather think the former.

A week later I was again at Fort William. I had arranged to accompany Fitz to a big cattle and horse fair the following morning. The majority of livestock in Ireland changed hands at fairs, although I preferred to buy store cattle at Ganly's auctions in Dublin. One had a much better selection and it did not take up the time that haggling and arguing over the price in a fair required. It could often take half an hour or more to conclude one deal! However, Fitz was convinced that cattle were cheaper in the fairs. He was probably right, providing one did not value one's time! I needed between forty and fifty good Hereford crossbred bullocks for grazing the paddocks at the Eaton Stud, so happily fell in with Fitz's plan.

Fairs were always fun, even if it was only watching the antics of the sellers, trying to squeeze a few more shillings out of a buyer who had made his final bid. The vendors expected prospective buyers to beat them down on the price, it was all part of a ritual. I quickly learned that on no account must one agree the first price asked, even if reasonable. The poor farmer would worry for weeks wondering if he could have got more for his cattle, but would go home happy even if he received anything from £5 to £10 less than his original asking price! I picked up Ben Lawlor and drove on to Fitz's house in Lismore. He was waiting outside. It was just 5.00 am. We quickly covered the short distance to the fair. As we left the car we were greeted by the customary noise, hustle and bustle of an Irish fair as bunches of cattle were driven into the town centre, to be held in their respective lots by a motley collection of drovers, owners and small boys anxious to earn a few pence; horses were showing their paces, being run up and down the main street to the accompaniment of much whip cracking and verbal encouragement.

With the aid of Fitz and Lawlor, I bought twenty-two good quality bullocks. I estimated the cost a little over £4 and 10 shillings per hundredweight. They were cheaper than in Dublin, but not that much. Leaving Lawlor to arrange transport up to Maynooth, Fitz and I, with the late owner of the bullocks retired to a nearby pub to complete the deal – the payment of a cheque. The vendor ordered up three large 'Paddys' – all part of the accepted custom. I'm not very keen on whiskey at 6.30am, but I gritted my teeth and took my medicine! It would have caused great offence not to have done so.

Our drinking companion, one Mick O'Hara, assured me he had twelve more equally good bullocks at home which he'd sell me, 'although begob you robbed me, so you did'. However, I declined and he left Fitz and me sipping our drinks – I was longing for a cup of tea! My companion suddenly gave me a nudge.

"Do you see those three men that have just come in?" I looked across the smoke-filled room.

"Yes, what about them?"

"Well, the taller one is the Duchess's uncle – Frank Sullivan."

I peered through the haze. Certainly one of the men, the taller, looked more distinguished than his companions, who looked like a couple of tinkers.

"I don't believe you."

"I can assure you it is. He's the naughty boy. The black sheep of the Sullivan family. Actually he's a hell of a nice chap to talk to. Mind you, I wouldn't trust him an inch as far as dealing with him is concerned, but then in this game he's not alone. He fiddles about a bit in horses, that is when he has any money. Would you like to meet him?"

The answer was a very firm 'no'. As the Duchess had never said anything about her Uncle Frank, I thought it wiser not to make his acquaintance. The mere fact that he'd never been mentioned would make it seem as though he was definitely *persona non grata* as far as the Westminsters were concerned. Soon after the spotting of Uncle Frank, Fitz and I left the fair.

I wondered at first about the Duchess having such a relation and then never gave the matter another thought until three years later, a few months after the Duke had died when I received a letter from the Duchess. It appeared that Uncle Frank had written a begging letter to the Duke, not long before the latter's sudden death and subsequently another one to his niece, Nancy. It seemed that Frank Sullivan was in debt to the tune of quite a few hundred pounds. He was in arrears with income tax, rates, was about to have the electricity supply cut off, had an overdraft at the bank, owed money to a number of trades people and those who, in the goodness of their hearts, had lent him money. The Duchess wished me to go and see her uncle and try and straighten out the mess. She was prepared to help him up to a limit of £500, but no more. Further, she had made it clear to her uncle, that this was a one-off happening.

I was not amused, I had more than enough work to cope with! However, I went down to Rushbrook just outside Cork and met Frank Sullivan at his home on 2 November. He was charming and most plausible. I remember thinking that he would sound most convincing if he were selling a horse to someone uninitiated in the ways of horse dealers!

We had a most pleasant and friendly meeting. He was in fact Mr Co-operation in person. He promised that he would obtain copies of all outstanding accounts – he admitted to throwing away most of them – and would forward them to me in Dublin. Absolutely no information would be withheld. He was so very grateful to dear Nancy, she always had been such a sweet little girl. I reiterated what the Duchess had already told him that, however much he was in debt, she was not prepared to advance more than £500. He assured me that he fully understood. I was, therefore, both amused and annoyed to receive a letter two days after our meeting, thanking me for being so helpful and understanding. His letter continued:

> 'I have been thinking over things, and owing to our conversation it struck me that with your approval if you get Nancy to agree to give me an extra £100 deposit, I would then be in a position if I saw a nice store horse to purchase him, and make him [break him in], which I can still do.'

There was no doubt that Frank was a trier! I passed on the suggestion to the Duchess, but she was not impressed. In fact she nearly abandoned the whole rescue operation. Next in the saga came a letter from Winifred Sullivan, the Duchess's mother. It was positively vitriolic on the subject of her brother-in-law. The following are a few quotations from her letter.

> 'Every large family has its black sheep – and he certainly qualifies for that position! For years he has overrun his income and applies to anyone he knows for money.'

One thing in the letter that made me smile was a reference to Frank's wife.

> 'She is organist at two churches in Cohb – for which she will be well paid.'

Obviously Winifred Sullivan was living in another world. The church of Ireland clergy received, on the whole, miserable stipends and all other emoluments made by the Church were on a comparable basis. I very much doubted if the unfortunate Mrs Frank Sullivan received more than ten shillings a service, if that!

Another extract reads:-

> 'My son absolutely agrees with me in thinking F.L.S. is quite unworthy of help – so do his brothers.'

The letter finished off:-

> 'F.L.S.'s whole family are fed up with him and I am very sorry that my daughter has taken up the matter.'

Finally there was a postscript.

> 'I dislike F.L.S. very much as you have gathered!'

The strange thing was that anyone I spoke to seemed to like F.L.S. (I never discovered what the L stood for) and accepted him for what he was – a cheerful likeable fellow, but a bit of a rogue at heart. Be that as it may, the net outcome was that it gave me a lot of work which, at the time, I could have done without. It was not until 25 January 1954 that I was able to report that F.L.S.'s affairs were finally straightened out – at least for the time being!

As implied in the opening paragraph of this chapter things were going apace in 1951 as far as 'Operation Death Duties' was concerned, but so they were in my personal life.

For reasons which were never totally clear to me, in the previous year I had been elected to the committee of the Fitzwilliam Lawn Tennis Club, Ireland's major tennis club, of which I was a mere bar member. Every year, a week after Wimbledon, it was the venue for the Irish Championship Tournament.

In Ireland everyone seemed to know one another. During tournament week this led to problems for the committee, when visitors, frequently close friends of a committee member, gatecrashed the member's bar and other facilities resulting in a number of complaints. It was decided that this behaviour had to stop. The question was who would be firm enough to see the wishes of the committee as a whole were implemented? Thanks to my, by then, very good friend, George McVeagh, the ball landed in my court.

One evening, having been on duty the two previous afternoons and evenings at the tournament, I was heading out of Dublin back to Bryanstown when I had a change of heart, turned and went back to the club. I entered the bar and there was one of my closest friends, Jim Ganly, drinking with a truly lovely girl. Without asking Jim I ordered a large G & T for me and conversation, which largely centred around field sports, continued. After another round Jim said he must go, then as an afterthought turned to me and said, "Do you know each other?'

I replied, "No, I only know this lovely lady is Tintie and she, presumably, after you using my name, must know I'm Michael"

Jim formally introduced us, "Cynthia Goodbody meet Michael Twist, a good friend of both George and mine. Land agent to the Duke of Westminster. Cynthia is always known as Tintie." With that he was gone.

I was well versed with the name Goodbody, for members of the family were involved in a leading firm of solicitors, stockbrokers and numerous other enterprises throughout Ireland. Tintie's sister Pam, had just gone on to the centre court, so we took our drinks and went out to the balcony to watch. I forget now who won, but I was to learn that both Pam and Tintie were excellent players. Indeed the following year they took more games off the great and delightful Little Mo Connolly partnered by Jean Walker-Smith, at that time England's number one, than any other pair that year in Europe.

As we watched I started to feel exceedingly hungry and suggested we went to the Russell Hotel for dinner. Tintie's face lit up and then said, "I can't possibly go to the Russell dressed like this." I had learned she was one of an elite few, forty-two to be exact, who were air hostesses with Aer Lingus. She'd come off a flight from Glasgow, changed into a comfortable skirt and blouse at the airport and come straight to Fitzwilliam to watch her sister play

"I'd never be allowed in dressed like this."

I laughed, told her not to worry, the Duke used the Russell a lot, in fact had recently referred to it, when talking to me, as 'the best little café in Europe'. As his agent it was part of my job, on the Duke's instructions, to generously tip the staff at Christmas – so no problem.

That evening was the start of a great friendship and the realization that we had many interests in common. I was to learn that she was very keen on golden retrievers and shortly after our first meeting made up her dog as the first champion of the breed in Eire. I too became very involved in this lovely breed – both showing and field trialing. I insisted, when we started the Bryanstown (our registered prefix) kennel, our dogs must not only conform to the Breed Standard, but must also be able to do the job for which the breed was developed – working gun dogs. This resulted at one time in our having three dogs in the kennel, all champions in the show ring and all winners of open field trials.

Our dogs have been an absorbing and enjoyable interest, making us many friends throughout the world. For years now we have both been Championship Show judges, both have judged our breed at Crufts and, even more importantly, bred and exhibited a dog that went Best of Breed at what is recognised as the greatest dog show in the world.

The friendship that developed that evening dining at the Russell quickly blossomed into a love that has lasted over fifty years. Cynthia's interest in the livestock on the estates I have managed has been equal to mine and far greater than that of 'The Owner'. We became engaged on the evening of Old Christmas Day (6 January) sitting in the car on the road overlooking a moonlit Killiney Bay, so frequently likened to the Bay of Naples and were married on 22 August 1951. Needless to say the Duke and Duchess were invited, but were unable to attend, but Ursula and Stephen were present, as were Ikey Bell and, of course senior members of the Duke's staff.

Tintie has often said she felt it was something of a miracle that the wedding took place at all in view of the stress I was under, which was once again causing blackouts. I was not alone, George Ridley was equally exhausted playing 'beat the death duties', but more of that later.

Ridley was to have flown over from Liverpool, early on Tuesday, the day preceding the wedding, to give him and me a chance to deal with a number of matters urgently requiring attention. Late Monday evening George telephoned to say he would not be arriving until late on Tuesday. The Duke, who was certainly *au fait* with the situation, for he and the Duchess had received an invitation to our wedding, said that he wished to see Ridley at 11.00am on the Tuesday to discuss various matters and then lunch with him at Eaton Hall. Consequently, I was to meet him at the Russell for a 'working dinner'.

I protested loudly. Explained that I had arranged a dinner party at Bryanstown, which included my best man and his wife, who were staying with me, my parents and several relations over from England. George was sorry, claimed he had explained to the Duke, but his interests must come first. He was sure that my friends and relations would have a pleasant evening, even without my company! I was not pleased. It was as well I had not planned a stag party. It was just on midnight on Tuesday when I eventually got back to Bryanstown.

The following morning, my wedding day, I spent an interminable time on the phone dictating to Honor Reveille, a job necessitated by my meeting with George Ridley the night before. On my way to church I spent three quarters of an hour in the Dublin office, signing letters and checking through figures. These George said, were urgently needed in the London office and could not wait until I had returned from my honeymoon. All this resulted in a mad rush and we passed Cynthia and her father less than half a mile from the church!

The Duke gave me a gold cigarette case as a wedding present. It would only hold five. I suppose it was good of him to give me anything, but it did not seem a lot, particularly when one took into account the many tasks I undertook for him which were far removed from the duties of a land agent. Time was to prove that it was indeed not a lot. In 1983 we decided to sell a lot of silver that Cynthia and I knew we would never use again. I had long since given up smoking and, as the case was not engraved, I decided to sell it. Its value to melt down as gold was £46! Not a very costly item, therefore, in 1951. On reflection it seems strange that he should have made such a trifling gift. He was not normally ungenerous. At the time I gave it little thought – we received a charming and congratulatory telegram on the day, which really meant a lot more.

I think that, of all the time I was with the Westminsters 1951 was *the* year – the one when it all seemed to be happening. Things were going well, permission had been granted to invest overseas – George Ridley was like the proverbial dog with two tails. This concession from the Treasury could lead to death duty evasion *par excellence.*

On 18 September a conference of agents and advisers was held at the London office. Ridley gave an opening address. He stressed that the social security and nationalization policies of the government had jeopardized the Stock Exchange market and would continue to do so. Under the current circumstances he felt that land would prove to be the soundest investment and the least threatened by Labour's policy of nationalization. This of course was nothing new, it had been his way of thinking since the start of 'Operation Death Duties'. He went on to say that the Duke's Stock Exchange securities had been reduced to a little over £1 million, which at their current value would show £250,000 profit if sold. The balance of securities had been sold to provide a profit of £750,000 – nearly all reinvested in agricultural properties.

It would become tedious to go into all the figures available, suffice to say that had the Duke dropped down dead at the time of the meeting, nearly a million pounds would have been saved through the agricultural policy. Ridley went on to inform us that, when he had become agent at Eaton in 1946, the Duke owned approximately 700 acres of commercial woodland. Thanks to the afforestation policy and the unceasing efforts of Langshaw Rowland, the acreage had now been increased to 9,000 acres – a source of great wealth for the Grosvenor family in years to come. However, it was hoped to at least double the area in the course of the next few years.

At this point I well remember George giving himself a little pat on the back. He paused, smiled broadly and said, "There is tremendous satisfaction in the knowledge that both with regard to our agricultural and forestry programmes we are making an investment which is of national as well as personal importance."

Ridley then gave a résumé regarding the London Estate. He explained that when he had become involved there were a number of problems – arrears of repairs, bomb damage and an ever-increasing demand for accommodation. The opportunities to obtain capital cash payments which passed to the trustees, and dilapidations monies which passed to the Duke had, he assured us, been considerable. He went on to clarify and enlarge on many points. His grasp of the legal loopholes in the tax system was almost uncanny. He was a brilliant and enthralling speaker and what could have become a boring and tedious address became, instead, an intensely interesting and fascinating exposition.

He paused, took what must have been a much-needed sip of water and continued to explain that upon the exhaustion of almost four-fifths of the trustee's investing monies and the whole of the latter's bank balance, ways had to be found to acquire further cash for future investment. He told us he had at first considered selling off a portion of the London Estate, but in the end had decided to keep the majority of it. Instead he and his fellow trustees had formulated a plan to grant long leases of up to 200 years on selected properties. This would produce large sums of money which would be equivalent to freehold sales.

Due to changes in the law this policy did produce some headaches for the 6th Duke some thirty or so years later, but at the time it appeared to be a brilliant scheme. It was to provide much-needed money for overseas investments. As far as ' Operation Death Duties' was concerned it had all the hallmarks of yet another example of Ridley's ingenuity.

Derek Turner, agent for the London Estate, appointed by Ridley several years before, with the full approval of the Duke, was a shrewd and dynamic personality. During the war he became a colonel and was on Viscount

Montgomery's staff when the latter was in command of the Eighth Army in North Africa. Derek was one of the members of the staff who had direct contact with His Grace. According to Bill Bryan, Derek had mildly 'blotted his copy book' when he had gone straight to the Duke over some matter and had bypassed George Ridley. However, at least on the surface, it did not appear to have caused any rift between the two.

Derek had been on 'safari' to South and East Africa looking for suitable investments in real estate, which had led to the purchase of a block of offices in Nairobi – the first step in developing the Grosvenor's overseas interests! The court had authorised expenditure up to £800,000 in Africa. Derek told the meeting that he had already found a London-based organisation prepared to lease the whole building.

While Derek Turner had been examining the possibilities in Africa, George Ridley, Langshaw Rowland and Tom Barty-King, one of the trustees and legal adviser to the Trust, had been on a similar mission to America and Canada. George's address lasted almost to lunchtime. As we walked across the road to Claridges, George told me that he was confident that Canada was where the Grosvenor millions could be saved and even more made. The trouble was, he continued, the bloody Treasury. They were, he said, so conservative in their approach to anything that it could take a lifetime to make them change their outlook. Our main problem was we hadn't got a lifetime!

George confided in me, as we sipped our gin and tonics, that he wasn't too happy about Africa. He did not believe, unlike his co-trustees, that the political situation in Africa would remain unchanged. He believed that independence and home rule was inevitable and long-term investment not a viable proposition as far as the trustees were concerned.

After lunch there was a long discussion on the merits of investment in Canada, Ridley was the most enthusiastic. A number of possibilities had been explored, but it was rather a case of window shopping, for until the Treasury relented little could be achieved. At least this was what we were led to believe to begin with, but Ridley said that there was a possibility – Annacis Island in the Fraser River, off New Westminster. Part of this, about half, was up for sale. It was owned by an English syndicate and there was a good chance that it could be purchased for sterling. Tom Barty-King explained how this could be done. Further, once we had a foothold in Canada there was far more likelihood that the Treasury would 'play ball' regarding the acquisition of the other portion of the island. He went on to explain that a causeway could be built to link the island to the mainland. Once this was done it would almost certainly become a valuable site for industrial development.

George Ridley then intervened, he told the meeting that the Premier and Cabinet Ministers for British Columbia were most enthusiastic over the proposed development and that they found the idea of a trading estate most attractive. Further that, once there was anything definite, they would approach the Dominion Government about building a causeway to link the island to the mainland.

At this point George digressed, from the serious business of the meeting, to recount an amusing little anecdote. At least amusing for everyone except Langshaw Rowland. He, together with George and Tom Barty-King, were attending a dinner party given by the Premier of British Columbia. The latter owned a Dalmatian dog; a great pet and much loved by its owner. They were all standing around, having pre-dinner drinks, when Langshaw suddenly felt something wet and warm on the back of his leg. He looked down to see the Dalmatian happily cocking his leg against his! With that Langshaw let out a roar as he pushed the dog none too gently away with his other foot.

The Premier smiled and said, "Clever, that dog of mine, Langshaw. He knew which man had to do with trees!"

Langshaw, George assured us, was not amused!

Numerous new tax benefits came to light during the course of the two days that the conference lasted. In addition there was much talk about death duties and how money could be raised to meet these when the time came. I remember it crossed my mind that, were the Duke to be privy to our discussion, he might have thought we were more interested in his demise, rather than that he should have a long and happy life. He'd have been wrong for, as George pointed out, the longer the Duke lived, the longer we had to cut death duties to a minimum!

There was, for me, one interesting revelation. £200,000 per annum of the Duke's personal money, as opposed to that of the trustees', was required to meet covenanted annuities. A lot of this went to ex-wives and old flames.

I returned to Ireland with instructions to look into the possibility of branching out into town property and the prospects of embarking on a large reforestation programme.

The Duke seemed in remarkably good form each time he came to Ireland. He let it be known that he had every intention of returning to Norway in 1952, to once again fish the River Alta, but this time it was to be in the grandiose style of the pre-war days. Namely, he wished to charter a yacht and sail to Bossekop using the vessel as a hotel. This had us all running around 'yacht hunting', looking for something suitable. Not easy to find, for the yacht would have to be large enough to withstand the roughest weather, have been awarded an Al rating at Lloyds and have a nice crew.

The charter was required from 13 June to 13 August. George Ridley had been in touch with Camper & Nicholson, they could only come up with two suggestions. Of these only *Radiant* was really suitable. However, when George heard the weekly charter rate the hunt was immediately on again. Something smaller and less expensive, he said, had to be found. It was all a waste of time. The Duke's yacht before the war, the Cutty Sark, had been built originally as a destroyer at the end of the First World War. She was over 260 feet long. The Duke wanted something of a similar class. Ikey told me that 'The Chief' had been quite testy about it and had told him that "Ridley wants me to go to Norway in a bloody dinghy!" So, as had been inevitable from the start, the *Radiant* was chartered. George wrote to me on 30 December 1951.

> 'Between you and me they are asking £1,500 per week for the *Radiant* and while I am all for seeing The Chief happy and comfortable even this figure rather staggers one.'

Twelve thousand pounds for eight weeks and that was only the yacht and crew. On top of that was the actual cost of the fishing, provisions and a good supply of drink. Using the same yardstick as I have applied to such things as agricultural properties, namely multiplying by forty, it works out at a somewhat costly holiday!

In 1951 the next in line for the title of Duke of Westminster was Captain Robert Grosvenor but he died most unexpectedly only days after the Queen's Coronation. That meant that Dorothy Mack's brother, William, became heir to the title. Next in the line of succession was Colonel Gerald Grosvenor, a truly delightful man, who eventually became the 4th Duke. Finally, his younger brother Robert. In 1951 there were no further male heirs. Robert was a man for whom I did not care; totally unlike his brother.

My feelings probably stemmed from an incident that occurred in the London office. I had just arrived and met Colonel Robert in the entrance hall. We were standing talking when the door opened and George Ridley entered. He looked frightful. He had, once again, been forced to take to his bed suffering from a severe bout of bronchitis. Robert Grosvenor did not ask if he was feeling better. George cracked some joke, to the effect that he'd been away so much of late that people would think he had resigned. Robert Grosvenor gave him an icy look and replied. "Any time you want to we'll be pleased to accept it." With that he turned and walked away. Poor George looked as though he'd been slapped in the face. Eventually he spoke.

"So much for working all hours to try and save their inheritance for them. If it wasn't for the Duke I'd let Robert and the rest get on with it."

However, it transpired towards the end of the year, just before Christmas, that Robert was not the end of the line. His wife, Viola, gave birth to a son, Gerald Cavendish, the current and 6th Duke of Westminster. He, I'm delighted to say, now has a son to carry on the family heritage.

9
Buy a Monument & Charter a DC10

George Ridley, Bill Bryan and Derek Turner visited Ireland in the early autumn of 1951. Derek's presence was purely a matter of familiarizing himself with the Irish properties. Bill was there as 'go between' – between Ikey and 'The Chief' – over the subject of dollars. It was an arrangement of which Ikey was tiring. He had found that he could get as much as fifty per cent more for his dollars than the official rate of exchange, which was all he received from the Duke. All had been well until Bend Or started teasing Ikey about how rich he was getting and what a fortune he, Ikey, was making out of his dollars. The latter was terribly upset over this and started asking some of his American chums how much they were getting for theirs on the Continent. What he learned caused him to become extremely agitated. Bend Or just laughed at him and told him that he was doing remarkably well and would not discuss the matter further.

We had done the round of the estates, arriving back in Dublin just before noon on a Friday. I had arranged that we should have an early lunch and then take a look at two properties which I thought admirably suitable as investments for the trustees. When we arrived at the Shelbourne there was a telegram for George. It was from the Duke, who was at Mimizan.

> 'Imperative that you, Bryan and Turner come at once. Westminster.'

I had never seen George so furious. He told us he had made it quite clear to 'The Chief' that come what may he was having the weekend off. He had made arrangements for him and his wife, Mary, to visit their two sons at their public school and that, George said, was what he was bloody well going to do. He wired the Duke accordingly, saying he'd be in Mimizan sometime on Monday and that Bryan and Turner were on their way. Both were as furious as George. They too had made arrangements for the weekend with their respective wives, whom they now had to telephone and cancel their plans.

Meanwhile I contacted Honor Reveille. She was able to get Bill and Derek on the only flight from Dublin to Paris, but we would have to rush. We just made it. Having seen our friends off, George and I lunched at the airport. He decided he would not bother to look at the two properties I had lined up, instead he said he'd catch the afternoon flight to Liverpool. He felt a night in his own bed would be more beneficial than bouncing around the Irish Sea for most of the night – he had originally been going back on the Dublin/Liverpool boat.

Quietly I cursed 'The Chief'. I had spent a lot of time and energy inspecting numerous properties, to whittle them down to the two I was so anxious that George and Derek should see. They looked to be really good investments and the maximum death duty rate in Ireland was fifty-three per cent, a saving of thirty-seven per cent on a similar investment in Great Britain.

It was Wednesday evening when Bill rang me – his language was inspired! On arriving in France he and Derek had, with difficulty, hired a car. They stopped just long enough at the airport to grab a sandwich and a quick drink, then set off for the Château Woolsack. They'd taken it in turns, driving flat out all the way. They had a puncture, and found the spare was soft. In fact, as Bill said, it had been a 'bloody awful journey'.

At last they reached their destination and were warmly greeted by the Duke. Both were relieved to find him in such good form, for, as they had raced across France, they had been speculating as to what could be so wrong as to require their immediate presence. It appeared that the Duke's guests for the weekend had had to call off. This meant that he and Nancy would be on their own and they wouldn't have a four for Canasta! The Duke had become most enthusiastic about the game. It was, apparently, to rectify this that Bill and Derek had cancelled their weekend plans and travelled almost non-stop from Dublin!

It was soon after this that a most disturbing happening took place. Derek Turner and I had become close friends. He had an exceptional brain, great drive and was, in fact, a most accomplished businessman. Further, he had no hesitation in standing up to Ridley, who had been showing signs of becoming somewhat autocratic.

One afternoon a letter arrived at the Dublin office marked 'Personal'. It had a Chester postmark. I opened it with some misgiving. It was from George Ridley, to say that, with the Duke's full approval, he had summarily dismissed Derek Turner. My first reaction was 'Oh no, not Derek, not Derek on the fiddle.' It was the only thing I could think of that could possibly lead to such action. He was so very much part of the team and obviously doing a splendid job. I read on, my surmise had been wrong. Lt. Col. D A Wetton-Turner MC had apparently been claiming an honour he had not received. He had never been awarded the Military Cross.

Someone, I never learned who, had filled in time looking up various people who had been awarded this distinction and Derek was not listed. Agreed, a very stupid thing to have done, but I always felt the punishment too harsh for the crime. Few people would have noticed if Derek had quietly dropped the MC after his name and in a few months the matter would have been forgotten. Whilst Ridley put the onus for Derek's dismissal squarely on the Duke's shoulders, I was to learn that Derek was by no means convinced of this. I was extremely upset by the whole business and, although it was contrary to implied instruction, namely, that no member of the Duke's staff should have anything further to do with Derek, I telephoned him that evening.

He was most appreciative of my call, agreed that it had been a totally stupid masquerade but swore he hadn't started it. Whilst in his previous job, with a top firm of London accountants, someone had added an MC after his name when writing to him. Foolishly he had not contradicted it. His secretary had noted it and started adding MC when typing his name and so the deception grew. Derek went on to say that he felt certain his dismissal was due to Ridley, not so much because of his stupidity over the Military Cross, but because George felt he was gaining too much influence with the Duke was after George's job. I remember he laughed and said "At least over that he would be right."

Derek told me that Bill Bryan had phoned him, as concerned as I was and had remarked that his cousin George was becoming 'a right little Hitler!' I could not agree. I found Ridley very easy to work with, receptive to ideas and appreciative of one's efforts. I just could not believe he would 'do the dirty' on a friend. Derek and his family moved to South Africa. We remained friends and regularly wrote to each other up to the time of his death a few years ago.

'Operation Death Duties' was progressing smoothly on all fronts. Bill Bryan had, in addition to his duties as 'secretary' to the Duke, been appointed as director and company secretary of Pulford Estates – the company dealing with forestry and the timber business. It seemed that George did not think Bill had enough to occupy his time! John Saunders, who I mentioned in an earlier chapter, had become Ridley's number one in Great Britain. He was doing a sterling job and gave George one hundred per cent support. In Ireland, on the forestry front, I thought I was making good progress. I had learned of an estate in Co. Offaly of just over 1000 acres, a very sizeable property for Eire. One of its main attractions was that it had just over 380 acres of standing timber, some nearly mature and a number of excellent young plantations, all well maintained. The care of the woodland far surpassed that of the agricultural land and there seemed no logical reason why the entire area should not be planted with trees. In addition to the main holding there were about three hundred acres of heather-bog, quite suitable for growing Sitka Spruce.

I walked the estate twice, even tested the reaction of senior people in government. My suggestion that the whole area should become woodland met with considerable support. I contacted Langshaw Rowland and asked him to come and inspect the property. He was, like me, most enthusiastic. Agreed that the asking price was extremely reasonable and thought we should go ahead. What did George Ridley think? I explained that I hadn't bothered him at this stage and had decided to put what would amount to a virtual *fait accompli* before him. Langshaw looked at me for a moment and then just said 'Ah.'

That night Langshaw stayed at Bryanstown with Cynthia and me. After dinner I telephoned George and gave him my news. To my amazement he was very lukewarm about the matter and, he said, most surprised that I had got Langshaw over before consulting him. I pointed out that at the September meeting I had been instructed to enquire into the possibilities of a large afforestation project in Ireland, a figure of 10,000 acres had been mentioned. Naturally, I had assumed that this meant I was to look for suitable locations, for this purpose. The outcome of a long telephone conversation was distinctly depressing from my point of view. The matter was to be left in abeyance for the moment. However, I was to continue to try to persuade the Devonshire Estates to sell the parcel of land, some 230 acres, across the river from Fort William – the Duke was still most anxious to acquire it. That night I lay awake for a long time thinking. I remembered what Colonel Devereux, my first employer, had said to me after receiving a report he had asked me to prepare.

"Michael, an excellent report, but you've made one mistake." I enquired what. "You've left nothing for me to say... Yes, but wouldn't so and so be better? Always makes a deliberate mistake, for the boss to pick up – that makes him feel good." Should I have left 'a deliberate mistake' for George? I'd never know, but he'd certainly dampened my enthusiasm for any Irish forestry project!

It was soon after this that Their Graces came over to the Fort. The morning they arrived I was on 'standby', in case I was wanted. As usual they breakfasted at the Shelbourne, but I received no summons. I wasn't too happy about this. Past experience had taught me that this could be the prelude to a rushed journey down to Lismore. I had only been there two days ago and the everlasting motoring was beginning to get me down. Three mornings later, I had just arrived at my office, when Honor Reveille came in with a telegram. It read:-

'Buy Wellington monument Trim. Move to Fort William. Re-erect in park. Westminster.'

I read it again, then handed it to Mrs Reveille. "Can you make any sense of this?" She read it, smiled and then said.

"Just a moment. There was something in yesterday's paper. I've still got it in my office." She returned a few minutes later.

"Here we are." She passed me the paper. There was a short report regarding a meeting of the Trim Council. One of its members, a staunch nationalist, had decided it was quite wrong that a damned Sassenach, the Duke of Wellington, should look down on their town.

'Look down' was indeed a very apt description, for the monument was very tall and very solid. It had, so I was told, steps up the inside of the column. Be that as it may, much heated debate had taken place which, according to the paper, led to the Council agreeing to sell it to the first person prepared to buy and remove it. Just then the phone rang. It was Ikey.

"Hello, have you heard from 'The Chief?"

"Yes, I received a telegram just a few minutes ago."

"Good, I had dinner with him and Nancy last night. Showed Benny the bit in the paper about the Wellington Monument..." And so it went on. I had learned that, not infrequently, when Ikey and 'The Chief' got together anything might happen! Ikey was usually the one with the 'bright idea', as he had been on this occasion. Anyway, the upshot of their little scheme was that Honor Reveille spent nearly an hour trying to track down the Clerk of the Trim Council. When at last she had him on the line, I explained the position and asked how much they were asking for the monument. Poor man, he seemed completely nonplussed by the question. Eventually he explained that he and, he truly believed, the majority of the Council never for one moment dreamed that anyone would be interested in buying the monument; further, that no final decision had been reached. I thanked him and extracted a promise that, if agreement to sell was ever reached, the Duke should have the first opportunity.

I then phoned Sisks and spoke to one of the directors with whom I had become very friendly. Did he know the Wellington monument at Trim? He did – well. I asked him what he thought it would cost to dismantle, move it to Fort William and re-erect it? He said he hadn't got a clue and had I been drinking? I assured him I was serious. Finally he believed me, said that he'd have a chat to John Sisk and ring me back within half an hour. He was as good as his word. He said he couldn't give me a definite price without going to Trim, but a very rough estimate was anything from £10,000 to £15,000. I sent off a telegram to the Duke.

'No definite decision Wellington monument. You have first refusal. Estimated cost of removal and erection £15,000. Twist.'

I heard no more!

On 8 February 1952 another meeting of the 'first eleven' took place at the London office. It seemed strange Derek not being there. George Ridley seemed in very ebullient mood. Great progress was being made with regard to selling 200-year leases. Those settled had already netted £2 million, whilst 'probables' and 'possibles' could bring in another £2 million. That he said was good, but the great news was that the trustees had been able to purchase half of Annacis Island. Apart from 'getting a foot in the door' in Canada, the great beauty of this deal was that it had been done for sterling. The purchase price was £40,000. Even better still was that negotiations were afoot to buy the remainder of the island. The likely price being £35,000. Further, a small freehold plot in Vancouver had been bought for £18,000. George had paused for effect, as I have said he was an excellent speaker, then he announced that all the purchases had been and would be in sterling. So, in spite of the opposition faced from the Treasury, the Grosvenors had a foothold in Canada and one that could not be aggregated with British interests for death duties.

There was more good news to come. A freehold block of flats had been purchased in Melbourne for £132,000. This left £370,000 still to invest in Australia. George stressed that the acquisition of suitable real estate was paramount. The Duke was not getting younger and whilst bricks and mortar, land and forests could not be moved to England to be added to his estate, cash most certainly could. Therefore, it was imperative to invest the £370,000 in real estate as quickly as was prudently possible. Further, it seemed that there were prospects for investment in the United States of America. George then returned to the subject of Annacis Island. He told us that a submission had been made to the Treasury for half a million dollars for the development of the island. This had the backing of Lord Ismay, Secretary of State for Commonwealth Relations, but he had stressed that it was the Treasury who had the final word.

That was all good news. The bad news was that Drummonds Bank had allowed a massive overdraft to accrue. They had asked George to call and see them at the beginning of the week. He had been horrified at the magnitude of the figure. It seems he had been so busy placing money beyond the grasp of the taxman that he had lost sight of where it was coming from. It crossed my mind that had Derek been behind his desk, at 53 Davies Street, this would never have happened. George continued on a more sombre note. Spending had to be cut to a minimum over the next four months. It was, he assured us, only a temporary hiccup in the general plan. However, he had undertaken to repay the bank £2 million of the sum outstanding by the end of June. It was obvious that the size of the overdraft was causing Ridley to have uneasy feelings, but he did not panic. Lesser men would have.

Just before leaving Ireland I had agreed the purchase of the land across the River Blackwater from Fort William, completing the deal over the phone with Fitz before I left for the airport. I had beaten him down to £18 per acre, £12 inside the limit George had given me! I asked George if this deal could still be completed, for as he well knew, it was something the Duke had been very keen on for a number of months. The answer was 'No.' No further expenditure meant exactly what he had said. I would have to delay the transaction until July. I was not happy. It seemed that everything I tried to do in Ireland was thwarted. When we adjourned for lunch, I walked to the restaurant with George. He said how sorry he was about the land at Lismore, but things were, purely on a temporary basis, impossible as far as further cash was concerned at the moment.

"What the hell am I to tell the Duke? He's always asking if I've bought it and getting quite testy when I tell him I haven't."

"You'll think of something." George stopped and looked me straight in the eyes. "But, whatever you say DON'T tell him that I've run up an overdraft with Drummonds of nearly £5 million. He'd have a fit." He gave a rather sickly grin. "That is unless you want to see me getting kicked out." That was unthinkable, but since then, I have often thought it a pity that I wasn't able to see into the future.

The situation with the bank was bad. During the afternoon Ridley asked Langshaw Rowland what were the possibilities of felling some timber now which had previously been earmarked to help meet death duties, and reduce the overdraft this way? Langshaw's reply was that at the moment the most that could be felled would only realise around £200,000 – a mere drop in the ocean.

George McVeagh was attending the meeting. We had put in much hard work to find suitable property investments in Dublin, as well as land for afforestation. McVeagh had also discovered a way for the trustees to avoid the twenty-five per cent stamp duty. In due course he put his ideas to the meeting regarding the latter, whilst I reported on a number of suitable properties I had inspected. We both received a very cursory hearing to our proposals. It had all been a waste of time, at least as far as the immediate future was concerned – the money well was, albeit temporarily, completely dry!

It was about two weeks later that I arrived in the Dublin office just after 2.00pm. Mrs Reveille seemed slightly agitated. She quickly explained that Richard Chapman had been on the phone – His Grace wished to see me immediately. I was to be at Bourdon House in time for dinner and stay the night. No problem, there was a flight to London at 3.30pm. However, when Honor Reveille telephoned Aer Lingus the flight was already fully booked. This was a most unusual happening in those days, but it was a Friday. I had, on several occasions in the past, noted that the Friday afternoon flight was frequently very full. It was nearly always due to preponderance of Roman Catholic Priests. Where they were going I never discovered.

"What have you done?"

"Subject to confirming it within the hour, I have booked you on the first flight out to London tomorrow morning. I did explain that it was most urgent. Couldn't they do anything today?" She paused and laughed. "They said the only thing they could do was to charter you a DC3, at a cost of £500." I too laughed.

"That certainly would be very ducal. I can just imagine travelling in splendid isolation, with the exception of a glamorous air hostess to look after me. What fun! To be serious, telephone Richard, explain the situation and say I'll be with His Grace by 11.00 am tomorrow."

I went through to my office, to deal with any letters requiring my attention. I had just settled down to my task, when the office intercom buzzed. I flicked the switch.

"Yes?" An almost breathless Honor Reveille gasped.

"His Grace is on the line."

"Right, put him through." I picked up the phone. "Twist speaking."

"Ah, yes, well, tell those aeroplane chappies to get that plane ready. See you in time for dinner."

The line went dead. It was the first time I'd ever spoken to 'The Chief' on the phone! I smiled to myself. The latter had no hesitation in expecting his staff to fly, but nothing would get *him* up in an aircraft. According to Basil Kerr, the Duke was terrified of flying – about the only thing he was frightened of. I buzzed Honor Reveille and told her to get on to Aer Lingus to see what time they could have the plane read by. Almost within seconds she was back to me, would I please speak to the man at the booking office, he didn't think she was serious, and neither did he believe me. It wasn't until I spoke to the Traffic Manager that the urgency of the matter was fully appreciated. He would ring me back and let me know when the plane was ready to leave. He added that, of course, the actual time of departure was entirely up to me.

I rang Cynthia, told her what had happened and would she pack an overnight case for me, not forgetting my dinner jacket and to bring it together with a change of 'city' clothes to me immediately at the office. She wasn't too pleased.

We were supposed to have been dining with the master of the local hunt that evening. I sat back in my chair. Working for the Duke had many compensations – but my own private flight, that really was something! I was enjoying myself, this was fun. It certainly beat having a first-class compartment reserved for me on the Holyhead/London train, as I had going home for Christmas after I had first moved to Ireland. The intercom buzzed. The Traffic Manager from Aer Lingus wished to speak to me, he said he had good news. There had been a cancellation on the 3.30 flight. He'd booked me on that, so there would be no need for me to charter a plane. What is some people's good news can be other people's bad! This, to me, was one of those occasions. I glanced at my watch. I certainly could not be at the airport in time to check in the usual thirty minutes before departure. I explained this and said that perhaps we should stick to the original plan. There was a long pause, then he said. "Not to worry. We'll hold the flight until 4.00pm." We took off at 3.55pm.

The Duke greeted me as though I was the one person he'd come to London to see, but then he always, well nearly always, exuded charm. The plane had been further delayed by a strong head wind and bad weather over the Welsh Mountains – the Duke had already changed for dinner.

"Come and have a drink, Twist, while Richard unpacks your bag and runs a bath for you."

We poured our drinks and went through to the library. It was only the second time I'd been in Bourdon House since my interview with Ridley in 1947.

"Tell you what I wanted to see you about – that forestry land at Lismore. What's happening? Hope you have bought it by now."

My mind raced. What the hell was I to say? Yes, but I can't close the deal because Ridley's run up such a vast overdraft with Drummonds that there is no money to pay for it. No, that would be landing a friend right in it and I looked upon George as being a very close friend. I had to lie, but I wasn't a very good liar. It is and was a trait that I deeply despise. I took a quick swig at my drink, I'm sure I was blushing as I replied.

"Well, I've made some progress, Your Grace. Lismore Estates are now prepared to consider selling it, but I rather fear, at an inflated price. They are having a meeting in June, after which they will give a definite answer. I have tried, but I cannot get them to budge from this position. Ridley had told me not to give more than £30 per acre. I'm waiting to hear their asking price, that is, of course, if they decide to sell."

"Hmm, not very satisfactory." Then, much to my relief, he smiled. "Keep at it, Twist. I want that land and don't worry about the price, buy it. Never mind what Ridley says. Now you'd better get changed, or you'll be late for dinner."

As I travelled back to Dublin, the next morning, I could not help thinking how much less tiring it would have been for me if the Duke had asked me about the land on the phone. But then that was not his way, if it had been, life would have become quite ordinary, possibly even mundane. So far, that it most certainly was NOT!

10
All Tax Liabilities Recoverable

To add to the fullness of life, I suddenly found myself with an additional responsibility. I was instructed to keep a watching brief on the Duke's grandson – Christopher Filmer-Sankey, Ursula's second son from her first marriage. Christopher was in his twenties and it seemed that he had three main interests in life – women, drink and horses. Christopher had first really come to my attention during a visit to the London office. I arrived for an appointment with George Ridley. When I entered his office I found him seething; I had never seen him so cross. It appeared that Christopher was in London, staying at Bourdon House. The Duke allowed his grandson to stay there if he wasn't in residence himself. That morning, a member of the house staff had gone to call Christopher and take him his early morning tea. The former entered the room and found Christopher in bed with not one, but two prostitutes he had collected off the streets! George had already contacted Sir William Charles Crocker, President of the Law Society and one of the Duke's legal advisers.

William Charles had been a friend of mine for a number of years, a delightful, but truly formidable character. He was both physically and mentally an awe-inspiring figure! He had originally made his name in insurance and had been responsible for the downfall of Leopold Harris – a notorious fire-raiser in pre-war days.

William Charles descended upon Christopher like the proverbial wrath of God and gave the young man the telling-off of a lifetime. Amongst many things he pointed out to Christopher that his behaviour could have led to one of the most costly acts of copulation of all times – although his phraseology was not quite so refined!

I did not give much further thought to young Christopher. I met him once or twice at Bruree, when visiting his mother. I was not impressed, for several reasons. He never looked one in the eye when he was talking and there was shiftiness about his general demeanour that would most certainly not inspire confidence. It was, therefore, with no great joy that I learned that Chris was getting married and coming to live in Ireland. Even worse was the fact that, as a wedding present, his grandfather was giving him a farm and the working capital with which to run it. I was to locate a number of suitable properties, vet them and, if I thought them suitable, arrange for Christopher to view them.

I took him around numerous studs and farms before he decided that Cooper Hill, some six miles out of Limerick, overlooking the estuary of the River Shannon, was his ideal. His bride to be, by then well forward in her pregnancy, according to Ursula, had no say in the matter. Cooper Hill, by Irish standards, was big – five hundred and fifty-three acres. A considerable amount of land reclamation work was required, but when completed it would be a very nice farm indeed. There was a large, Georgian-style house, most attractive and a superb view across the river. It seemed to have everything the young couple could possibly want. Liz, Chris's wife-to-be, was equally horse mad; they had so much in common! It was not difficult to picture the idyllic life they could make for themselves, a lovely home and, if they were sensible, no money worries. However, 'The Chief' while prepared to see his grandson comfortably settled obviously had reservations. The property was to be held in trust.

Once the newly weds had moved in, I was instructed to pay fortnightly visits. Ostensibly to give advice if asked, but in reality to keep a watching brief. When I purchased the property I persuaded the vendor to include all the farm machinery and a small herd of pedigree Hereford cattle in the agreed price. One cow in the herd was particularly good – a first prize winner at the Royal Dublin Society's Spring Show and the dam of a young bull that had realized a very high price at the Dublin bull sales. A bull calf out of this cow would be worth anything from 50 to 100 guineas at a week old. Whereas, one out of any of the other cows, would not fetch more than 25 to 40 guineas at the same age.

On one visit to see the Filmer-Sankeys around the end of March, Christopher took me off to see his super cow and her newly born bull calf, and a very fine one it was too. Chris seemed delighted and said how thrilled he was with his Herefords and that he felt sure, if he looked after them properly, they would make him plenty of money. I was quite encouraged by such enthusiasm. Could it be that the prodigal was turning over a new leaf?

It was about six weeks later that I received a phone call from the secretary of the Hereford Herd Book Society in England. To be classified as pedigree, all young stock had to be tattooed in the ear with identifying letters and numbers and registered with the Society by the time they were a month old. The secretary apologised for worrying me, but would I confirm that Mr Christopher Filmer-Sankey of Cooper Hill, Limerick was the Duke of Westminster's grandson. I told him that he was right in his assumption, was there anything wrong? It appeared that there was, something very wrong.

Chris had duly registered the bull calf out of his good cow and over the next five weeks he had registered four more bull calves, all purportedly from the same cow! The secretary was most concerned in so far that he did not wish to do anything that might embarrass the Duke. It was obvious that all five registrations would have to be cancelled, but it was eventually agreed that the heifer calves, from the other cows that Chris had registered should be accepted. There was one condition – the herd should be dispersed as quickly as a sale could be arranged. From then on Christopher was definitely *persona non grata* with the Hereford Herd Book Society. Cursing volubly, I departed to Limerick.

Christopher was quite unruffled. Even when I pointed out that he might well find himself in court for obtaining money under false pretences. He did, however, say he was surprised that he had been found out and he couldn't see what all the fuss was about. One cow was much like another. I told him that I would want the names and addresses of all the people to whom he'd sold calves and the money back to refund them. He roared with laughter at the latter suggestion and said it had all gone, mostly on a new potential steeplechaser. Then with a big grin he added. "I've a bloody great overdraft at the bank too. I told them who I was and, of course, grandpa being who he is there was no question of any collateral being required."

It was time to take a firm stand. I telephoned Fitts, the auctioneers in Limerick, and arranged for one of the partners to meet me at Cooper Hill the next morning. I also made an appointment to meet Chris's bank manager later in the day. I then went to the Dunraven Arms in Adare and booked in for the night, where I phoned Ridley. He was upset, to put it mildly. He agreed completely with my plans and fully endorsed my suggestion to utilise the proceeds from the sale of the Hereford herd to clear Chris's overdraft. The next day when I saw the bank manager I told him the overdraft would be cleared, but that the Duke most certainly would not guarantee Chris's financial arrangements in future. This I confirmed in writing as soon as I returned to Dublin. I visited all the people who had bought bull calves from Christopher and refunded their money, with cheques from the Bruree account. Further, I told them they could keep the calves as recompense for the trouble they had been caused. Christopher thought the whole incident one big joke and neither he nor Liz showed the slightest animosity towards me for forcing the sale of the herd.

The main farming enterprise at Cooper Hill was buying in store bullocks in the early spring, fattening them through the summer and selling them in the autumn as beef. It was good land and, in a normal year, one could comfortably turn over 250 to 300 head, showing an increase in value of £15 to £20 per beast. I had arranged, through a most reliable cattle dealer, to buy in Shorthorn bullocks from Co. Clare, weighing around eight hundredweight and which should fatten out at around ten and a half hundredweight.

That was the end, at least as far as Christopher was concerned, of Cooper Hill. Munster & Leinster Estates took over the property, at cost, from the trustees. A small house, with about twenty-five acres of land was bought for Christopher in Co. Kildare. The difference in the sale price of Cooper Hill and the purchase price of Kildare house, together with the sum realised for the nondescript collection of cattle that Christopher had acquired was invested and put in trust, thus providing him with a moderate income.

Once the Filmer-Sankeys had left Cooper Hill, the newly appointed steward removed a medium-sized tractor trailer load of empty bottles from the house and took it to the Limerick refuse tip – the majority were 'Gordon's' gin bottles! Christopher continued his 'winning ways' once he had settled in Kildare, but at least I had not far to go when I had to intervene in some of his less endearing activities! Sadly Christopher died at a very early age, still in his twenties, from a brain tumour. Truly a short life and a full one. He was totally different from his elder brother Patrick, who was hard working. When I met him at Bruree on various occasions, while he was visiting his mother, I always found him to be both intelligent and charming.

The 24 April saw me, yet again, in London for another meeting of the Duke's top executives and advisers. The overdraft scare seemed to have subsided. It was, once again, full steam ahead with 'Operation Death Duties'. Ridley reported that the second half of Annacis Island had been purchased, but,unfortunately not for sterling. However, after a considerable battle with the Treasury, they had granted permission to acquire sufficient dollars to purchase the remainder of the island.

George had been right in his misgivings regarding the suitability of investments in South Africa. The political situation was worsening. He had therefore decided to transfer £500,000 from Johannesburg to Nairobi and to look for suitable investments in Kenya. He then went on to discuss general finances and to say that the overall position had very much improved, particularly in respect of tax relief, which could be listed under four headings.

1. Schedule D, which embraced both farm and forestry activities and from which one could gain almost immediate tax relief on any losses.

2. Maintenance claims on buildings, which provided relief over a period of five years.

3. Capital improvements on agricultural estates.

4. Covenanted annuities.

So successfully and skilfully had these opportunities been exploited, that a time had come when discretion had to be exercised. An almost unbelievable situation had arisen where, should the current policies be pushed to their limits, the whole of the Duke's tax liability would be recoverable! That, George said, could lead to a situation not wholly acceptable to the Inspector of Taxes, who might decide to bring about some serious adjustments to the tax laws! Under the circumstances we would have to show restraint and leave a respectable margin to swell the coffers of the Inland Revenue. It was a case, to as small a degree as possible, of rendering unto Caesar that which is Caesar's however painful this might be!

Ridley paused to let the full implication of his words sink in. Langshaw Rowland was the first to speak. He looked at George and then laughing said, "You are either the greatest fiddler of all time, or the greatest genius. I favour the latter. To create a situation whereby, through the manipulation of the tax laws and the juggling of vast sums of money, the wealthiest man in Great Britain need not be liable to income tax is, indeed, nothing short of sheer genius." Langshaw looked around the table, shook his head and continued. "Too rich to tax! Gentleman, I think a round of applause is called for." It was readily given.

It was quite remarkable that one man, George Ridley, ably supported by a team of loyal enthusiasts, should have contrived a policy whereby a situation could be reached, if so desired, where the wealthiest man in Great Britain need not pay any Income Tax! What was even more remarkable was the fact that this position had been achieved in strict adherence with the laws of the country.

The overall policy continued to be threefold: namely, to reduce death duty liability on the Duke's estate to a minimum; maintain income, so as to obtain the maximum tax relief which it was thought would be acceptable, and to make sound investments abroad that would not only reduce the death duties payable in Great Britain, but also ensure the future wealth of the Grosvenors.

Geoffrey Singer, the estate surveyor, a staunch ally of Ridley and now responsible for all lease negotiations on the London Estate, reported on the financial situation. It was markedly improved, but, he informed the meeting, there were no prospects of raising £5 million by June to wipe out the overdraft with Drummonds. However, the agreed £2 million would be available. Since the last meeting more than £1 million had been received for the sale of the Southern Estate, together with nearly £1/2 million for a freehold sale. In addition documents were in the process of being prepared for the sale of over £1 million in long leases. It now seemed likely that, in addition to the anticipated annual income from rents of £1 million, the estate might reasonably expect a further £3 million from other sources for the year ending 30 September 1952.

The clampdown on expenditure imposed at the

previous meeting, had been shortlived. Geoffrey Singer and John Saunders had been over to Ireland to inspect two properties I had located in Dublin. Unfortunately, in the case of the lesser of the two, the vendor had discovered who I was and had literally doubled the asking price. I was not amused and immediately broke off negotiations. However, the second building was far superior and appeared to be an excellent investment. It was a block of seven shops on the corner of South Anne Street and Grafton Street above these were three floors of offices. The majority were already let, subject to the satisfactory completion of the building. Geoffrey Singer agreed that it would be a good investment and after some discussion, I was told to negotiate a price and report back to the next meeting. At last it seemed as though something was going to happen on the real estate front in Dublin. I returned to Ireland feeling very elated, for not only had I the go ahead for the South Anne Street property, but I had been told to close the deal for the land across the river from Fort William. George had authorized this after the meeting.

The Duke and Duchess had crossed to Ireland the night before I returned. The former knew I was in England and I fervently hoped that I would not receive a call and have to go racing off to Lismore. The weather was incredible, more like high summer than April. There were a mass of items requiring urgent attention, but I gave priority to a request from the estate agents for the South Anne Street property for an early meeting. I arranged it for 3.00pm the following day. I planned to fly back to London the day after to inspect a consignment of Jersey cattle that Harry Hobson & Co, one of the country's leading pedigree livestock auctioneers, had put together for me. If I caught the 'Early Bird' plane, had a car waiting for me on arrival and returned on the last flight I could do it in the day.

That evening when I returned to Bryanstown I told Cynthia my plans. She was not amused, as she said, with a good deal of justification, she had seen more of me when we were engaged than she did now we were married. The formation of a Jersey herd was my idea, frowned on by Ridley, but approved by the Duke. The point was that Jersey milk realised nine pence a gallon more than Shorthorn milk and was in great demand.

I arrived in the Dublin office before Honor Reveille. I telephoned Fitz to close the deal on the land. He was silent for a moment and then said. "You're not going to like this. You've missed your opportunity. The Duke (the Duke of Devonshire) has changed his mind and has decided not to sell." I was furious. There was Ridley spending tens of thousands all over the world, but when required, particularly a few weeks ago, there weren't the £4,000 to buy something the Duke particularly wanted. I told Fitz to see if he could persuade the owner to change his mind, but he seemed to think it unlikely. The morning flew by and I had just returned to the office after lunch when there was a phone call from Fort William.

The Duke wished to see me most urgently and I was to stay the night. This meant leaving immediately and cancelling my 3.00pm meeting with the estate agents as well as my trip to England. I had to leave it to Mrs Reveille to do this, as I rushed back to Bryanstown to pack an overnight bag. I knew there was no point in phoning Cynthia, for she had been going to lunch with John Houston, of film fame and his delightful wife Riki. John rented Courtown, in the neighbouring parish of Kilcock, a palatial Georgian house which he used as a retreat, where he could relax and in the winter indulge in one of his favourite pastimes – fox hunting. It was through the latter that we had first met.

I hastily packed, scribbled a note to Cynthia, which I left with Mrs McManus, who was still with us as our cook/housekeeper, and departed for Lismore.

By present-day standards it wasn't far from Bryanstown, only 142 miles, but the quality of the roads was such that one was really pushing it to average much more than 35 mph. It was just after 3.00pm when I left Maynooth and I arrived at Fort William at exactly 6.45pm. The Duke met me in the hall. There were none of the usual pleasantries, no preamble.

"Bloody tradesman raced passed the front of the house just after lunch, nearly ran poor old Dringalo over. I want a second avenue, immediately, so these damned vans don't come tearing past. Damned fellow nearly killed my dog."

I made suitable sympathetic noises and said I'd get onto the matter the first thing in the morning. Apparently that was not good enough.

"Didn't get you to come down here, Twist, to leave it until tomorrow. I want something done tonight." With that he turned and walked away. Fortunately I had Michael O'Driscol's private number. He was now a director at the Cork branch of Sisks and was virtually in charge. I was lucky and caught Michael at home, so I quickly explained the problem. Protesting loudly, he finally agreed to meet me at Fort William at 8.00am the next morning. It was about sixty miles from Cork, which by normal Irish standards meant an early start for O'Driscol.

Next I contacted Fitz. Had he heard about the alleged speeding past the front of the house? He had. The lad from the Lismore Wine Vaults had been making a delivery, as the house came into view he saw the Duke sitting outside the front door, sunning himself and enjoying his after-lunch coffee. When he saw the Duke the poor fellow didn't know what he should do, go back, continue but stop when opposite the Duke, get out and bow, or creep past in bottom gear, pretending he hadn't noticed His Grace. He opted for the latter. However, he admitted that once past the Duke he had accelerated. He had seen a little dog, four or five yards away from the Duke, sniffing about on the gravel. The driver was adamant that he crawled by a good ten to fifteen yards from the dog.

I explained to Fitz that another avenue was to be

constructed immediately. It would, like the main one be nearly a mile long – a very costly job starting from scratch, however, Fitz provided some interesting information. He told me that the original driveway to the house had come in through a belt of trees on the western boundary. Further, he thought that we would find a sufficiently hard base that, once cleared of briars and other rubbish, would be sound enough to lay tarmacadam on without incurring the very considerable expense of having to put in a foundation. This was certainly good news. I phoned O'Driscol again and told him. I also suggested that he should arrange to have a foreman and one or two labourers on the site first thing in the morning. They could start clearing the old avenue and His Grace would see that his wish was receiving immediate attention.

Fitz proved to be right. An army of men went to work and in less than three weeks the 'tradesman' entrance was complete. It cost £4,500, the equivalent of about £180,000 at current rates. It was never used, except when the Duke was in residence and then only because Fitz reminded all the trades people in Lismore to do so. An expensive whim. It was ironic that the wretched Dringalo died shortly after the new avenue was completed!

It was early the following week and I was once again about to go to England to inspect Jersey cattle, when I received an SOS from Ikey. He and the Duke urgently wanted some extra large rubber bands to use as catapults! They had made paper ammunition, folding strips of paper into V shapes then, having cut one end, held the open end of the paper with their teeth and then stretching the elastic band they shot, or attempted to shoot flies, moths or any other target they could spy. This I gathered, was an after-dinner frolic when the port had been round a few times. Ikey stressed that he felt it important that I, personally, should select the bands. Subsequently, after the Duke's trip to Norway, I received a letter from Ikey in which he referred to the elastic bands.

> 'The Chief' told me that he had never had fun in his life with them while in Norway and he never had such splendid ones.'

All of which proves two things. Firstly, a resident land agent's duties are both varied and limitless and secondly, that even a Duke can behave in a juvenile manner!

11
No Cabins? Then Buy the Shipping Line!

It was early in 1953 that I received a telegram from the Duke.

> 'Have you bought land across river from Fort William? Westminster.'

I replied immediately. 'No. Owner will not sell. Twist.' But, how to explain the situation fully? If I told the truth George Ridley would certainly be in trouble, but if I didn't I could be the one to get the blame. I had told George several months ago that the opportunity had been missed. I had also assumed that he would have told the Duke, but it was clear he had not done so. Eventually, I decided to compromise. I wrote to 'The Chief' apologising for not having kept him informed, but saying I had notified Ridley of the position and had assumed that he would pass on the information.

Evidently this explanation was accepted. I never heard another word about the land from either His Grace or Ridley. It became clear that by 'covering' for Ridley I had in no way 'blotted my copy book'. I was dining with Ikey, about ten days after I had written to the Duke. He showed me a letter he'd had from Bend Or, mostly on the subject of dollars, but in the last paragraph he'd written. 'So pleased with the work Twist is doing, don't know what I'd do without him in Ireland'. It was nice to get a pat on the back, even if indirectly and I was obviously not being held responsible for the loss of the land.

There was much activity at the beginning of the year, it saw the ownership of the Bruree Stud transferred from Munster & Leinster Estates to Lady Ursula. It also saw the development of a stud at Bryanstown. Half the mares were to be moved to the new premises at Maynooth, the remainder were to be returned to the Eaton Stud. It was all rather complicated and, I thought, foolish. My reason for thinking that was quite simple – one paid virtually no Income Tax on profits made from bloodstock in Ireland, but one paid the full amount in England.

The removal of the mares from Bruree generated a good deal of ill feeling, particularly with Stephen Vernon. He took it as a personal condemnation of his ability to manage the stud and in this he was correct. He strongly disapproved of my being responsible for the mares at Maynooth and was equally adverse to Beedleston, the stud groom, moving to Bryanstown with them. Ursula had somehow, not through me, learned that Munster & Leinster Estates was a company set up in name only and belonged to all intents and purposes to the Duchess. To begin with she was very sour. However, she had a definite objective – the ownership of Bruree House and the stud. To achieve this she put on a front to appease her father, although she had no great love for his fourth wife, years younger than she. (This she made abundantly clear to me on numerous occasions, but it was nothing compared with her dislike of George Ridley! However, she was more than prepared, to play up to him or indeed anyone else to get what she wanted.)

Once it was established, that money would be released from her Trust, to buy her home from Munster & Leinster Estates she became all honey and sweetness. Once the property had become Ursula's, Stephen was again friendly and delighted to see me. Now that Bruree was no longer my responsibility I quite often spent a night there with Ursie and Stephen when visiting Cooper Hill – I had a very soft spot for Ursula.

'The Chief', meanwhile, did not lose his touch as far as finding unusual and difficult jobs for me. Nearly always these were, in the main, one of Ikey's brainwaves. It was through the latter that the Duke learned that there was a small Irish shipping line, operating out of Cork. Their main business was between their homeport and various ones along the French coast. The ships were small coasters, carrying merchandise and a limited number of passengers.

One port of call was not far from Mimizan. His Grace, undoubtedly encouraged by Ikey, decided what fun it would be to go to France on one of these little coasters, which were little more than tramp steamers. With his usual enthusiasm he instructed Richard Chapman to phone the company and find out when the next sailing was. It was in eight days' time. The Duke was delighted and told Richard to ring back and book him, the Duchess and his normal entourage on the next boat. However, all the accommodation was taken. A company spokesman said how sorry they were. Much as they would have been honoured to have Their Graces as passengers, it was impossible. That was when I spoke to 'The Chief' for the second and last time on the telephone. He rang me, or to be more accurate, Richard rang me to say the Duke wished to speak to me. It was one very cross peer that came on the line. He made it very clear that he intended to be on the next sailing that left for France. I was to arrange it, buy the company if necessary.

It was a repeat of the Munster & Leinster Bank charade – but this time it was to prove to be much more trouble. It took me ages to contact the managing director of the company and when I told him what I wanted he was not amused, in fact he was downright rude. Who the hell did the Duke of Westminster think he was? I replied the richest man in the British Isles and one of the wealthiest men in the world, who would, if necessary, buy the shipping line to get what he wanted. The reply was of such a nature that it is certainly not printable. I persevered, but it was obvious that it was not going to be an easy or quick job. He hung up once more, but I rang back.

Eventually, he said. "You're not going to take no for an answer are you?" I told him that at last he was getting the right idea. There was silence, then, "All right. I'll cancel the existing bookings on once condition?" I asked what it was, the reply was immediate, "You pay treble the normal fare, in advance." I readily agreed, it would be a lot cheaper than buying the shipping company!

The day of departure arrived. The luggage stored in the cars, with an extra car or it may even have been two, hired to take the staff. Jim Willoughby, the chauffeur, told me later that His Grace was in excellent humour as he climbed into the car in front of Fort William. As the cortege moved off the sun was shining, it was, in fact, a really glorious morning. They reached the road and, suddenly, His Grace told Jim to stop. According to the latter, the Duke looked around, laughed and, turning to the Duchess said.

"It's lovely here. I think we'll stay a few more days. Turn around, Willoughby and go back to the house."

Richard Chapman phoned me shortly after and gave me the news. Having confirmed that this was absolutely definite, I rang the managing director of the shipping company. His language was magnificent! I have seldom known anyone more angry. He swore and cursed for about five minutes. Finally he said "He's not bloody well having his money back." I assured him that there was no thought of that. He calmed down at once, in fact he became quite friendly and said he'd been doing a lot of thinking since first we'd talked. Did the Duke still want to buy his company and why had His Grace changed his mind at the last moment?

I replied that the Duke was no longer interested in buying the company. As to his second question – well the sun was shining at Lismore! With that I hung up. I'm sure the poor man thought I was mental, on second thoughts, he probably thought the whole ducal set up was distinctly peculiar. There were times when I would have wholeheartedly agreed with him!

Early in the year Ridley called a further meeting of 'the first eleven'. There was a new member to the team, Sir

Bernard Blatch. He had recently retired as solicitor to the Inland Revenue and was now being employed, by the trustees, on a consultancy basis. It was typical of George Ridley's foresight that he should have acquired the services of Blatch with his inside knowledge to help him negotiate with the Inland Revenue authorities. Blatch's appointment was not entirely popular, particularly with Bill Bryan. According to him, Sir Bernard was receiving a retainer of £10,000 per annum. Bill thought this excessive when compared with the remuneration which we received and the unlimited hours we were expected to be on call. I have no idea whether Bryan was right and really did not worry about it, but I did appreciate what a shrewd move it was on Ridley's part.

George gave his usual opening address – a résumé of what had been happening since the last meeting. When he came to Annacis Island he waxed almost lyrical over its potential. It was, he assured us, another Mayfair in the future of the Grosvenor family.

Gilbert Hardman, who had been appointed as agent in Canada, was, George told us, doing a superb job. Just twenty-eight when he went out there from London, he was a veritable 'whiz kid'. He was currently involved in laying on the required services, to the proposed two-hundred-acre factory site – electricity and water. The causeway was being built, road and rail links were being developed. All, it seemed, was rosy on Annacis Island with one exception – every rose has a thorn! In this case it was an aged Chinese man, the owner of a strip of land in the centre of the island. He proved to be a shrewd negotiator, although perhaps obstinate would have been a better description. He sat tight and no way would he accept the price paid to a number of fishermen who had had smallholdings on the Island. He was wise enough to realize all he had to do was remain calm and stick out for his price. By doing so he could delay the development and consequently cost the Duke a lot of money. Eventually much to the Duke's amusement, George had to agree to the old man's price. It was the only time I ever knew him bested!

Tom Barty-King told the meeting that he was in the throes of negotiating with the Bank of England for the $11/2 million dollars required for the development of the island. So great were the possibilities, that he felt he must suggest to the meeting that it might well be necessary to take someone in Canada into partnership to share the responsibility of maximising the full potential of the project.

George Ridley then went on to the subject of general finances. Smiling, like the proverbial 'Cheshire Cat', he informed the meeting that we had arrived at a quite extraordinary situation, for, in spite of his previous warning, we had reached a stage where the Duke would be entitled to recover ALL the tax that he paid. It was an almost unbelievable state of affairs. It was, also, a factual tribute to George Ridley's amazing ability. After a considerable amount of chat, it was decided that Sir Bernard Blatch should consider, very carefully, what possible repercussions the full implementation of this unique position might have on the future. The general opinion was that it might be diplomatic to forego certain tax reliefs, at least for the present. I well remember thinking that, as far as Sir Bernard was concerned, it was surely a case of gamekeeper turned poacher!

I was able to report that a price had been successfully negotiated for the Grafton Street property in Dublin and that a contract was being prepared. It was 'small fry' compared with Annacis Island, but it was another link forged in 'Operation Death Duties'. I returned to Ireland feeling that, at last, all my hard work in connection with real estate in Ireland was going to pay off.

I had only been back home for twenty-four hours when Ridley phoned me. Once again 'the almighty dollar' was becoming a bone of contention between Ikey and 'The Chief'. I was to go to Lismore at once and get things straightened out with Ikey. I protested that I really didn't want to get involved in the Duke's dubious currency transactions, but I had little choice, it was an order.

When I reached Fort William, Ikey was waiting for me. I had asked him to dinner, feeling the problem might be more easily solved over a pleasant meal. Poor Ikey, he was in a terrible state. He produced figures and a letter from his American lawyer, Marty Candler, which showed that since Ikey had started supplying Bend Or with dollars he had transferred over £70,000 worth from the States. The figures went on to show that Ikey was owed nearly £10,000. Benny, Ikey assured me, sometimes did not realize that everyone was not as wealthy as he was and that being owed such a sum was causing him much worry and distress.

I reported back to Ridley and sent a copy of the lawyer's statement to him, to show the Duke. Presumably George passed the information on to His Grace. I did not pursue the matter further; I just didn't want to know. However, ten days later, when I again visited Fort William and dined with Ikey at his home, I found he was greatly cheered. He was, once again, all smiles at the mention of his dear friend's name and full of the fact that he would do anything for him.

On 1 June, Cynthia and I flew over from Dublin to London, the Queen's coronation was the next day. We were staying in a flat in Upper Brook Street, in one of the Duke's properties. It was on the ground floor, quite small, with just one bedroom. The first floor was a spacious and very comfortable flat, occupied by George Ridley and there was a married couple, supplied by the estate, to look after him and to act as caretakers for the rest of the building. Bill Bryan had phoned me some days earlier. Would Cynthia and I mind if he, his wife Betty and their daughter Anne 'camped' in the sitting room? The answer was of course, 'the more the merrier'. It would be cramped, but it was of little consequence!

We all went out to dinner together to a nightclub, and eventually walked back to Upper Brook Street, having joined in the merrymaking that pervaded London that night. We did not retire until 3.45am on the morning of 2 June and were up again in time to walk down to Bourdon House to see the Duke and Duchess leave for Westminster Abbey at 7.00am. Both looked magnificent in their robes and full regalia as a peer and peeress of the realm. A few other members of the staff were present and we gave Their Graces a hearty cheer as they drove off. We returned to Upper Brook Street, had a traditional British breakfast of bacon and eggs and, because it was Coronation Day, washed it down with champagne!

We watched the ceremony at the Abbey on the television in George's flat, then made our way round to Park Lane. Here, at one of the Westminster properties together with other members of the Duke's staff we enjoyed the lavish hospitality of 'The Chief'. A magnificent cold buffet had been laid on, which included salmon from Lochmore and unlimited champagne. We had a superb view of Her Majesty and the procession as it passed. Truly a day to remember, made all the more wonderful by the Duke's generosity.

It was not long after the Coronation that the Duke again took off for Norway, to once more fish the River Alta. *Radiant* had again been charted from Lord Illiffe and, as for the previous trip, first came to Ireland to be provisioned. This was done with all the usual rush and urgency that I now automatically associated with the Duke's requirements; it was alas, to be for the last time. *Radiant* returned to Scotland on 16 July, after the Duke had had a happy, but strenuous, time fishing his beloved Alta.g

Subsequently, I was told by a member of the household staff that the Duke was very tetchy the next day. Not at all his normal cheerful self. Three times he went down to the River Laxford to fish. On one occasion he insisted, against the advice of his head gillie, on fishing a stretch of the river which normally they did not bother about. He caught a salmon and, it seems, was very bullish over it with the gillie.

That night, 17 July, he had a very severe heart attack. A doctor was urgently summoned from Lairg. The latter having examined the Duke, thought a second opinion should be sought and fully supported the Duchess's suggestion that the Duke's friend and doctor, Dr Rossdale, should be asked to come posthaste from London.

George Ridley was on his way to Lochmore when he received news of the Duke's sudden illness, he arrived at his destination on the evening of the 18th. Dr Rossdale had confirmed the extreme gravity of the situation and had told the Duke that, for the present, he must not move and should be prepared for a protracted period in bed, to be followed by a lengthy convalescence.

George Ridley told me that he saw the Duke soon after he arrived at Lochmore and had little doubt but that 'The Chief' was fully aware of the situation. Nurses had been brought up from London by Dr Rossdale, there was to be one on duty all the time. On the evening of the 19th, so I was told, when the rest of the household were at dinner, the Duke instructed the nurse to go down to the library to fetch him several books, when she returned, minutes later, he was dead. Bill Bryan phoned me late the following evening. He had been talking with his cousin, George. Apparently, in the nurse's absence, the Duke had got out of bed. Was it foolhardiness or was it intentional that the Duke flouted the doctor's orders? No one will ever know. Certainly no one could have wished such a vital personality a lingering end as a wholly, or partially, bed-ridden invalid.

Ridley phoned me later that evening to tell me the shattering news and to say that it was imperative that I go to Bruree, to be there early in the morning, to break the news to the Vernons before they heard it on the wireless. I felt numb with shock as I drove mile after mile through the deserted countryside. It seemed impossible that 'The Chief' was dead. He was a legend, surely he could not die? There would never again be instructions to buy a bank, or a shipping line; no more racing around to satisfy the smallest whim. Yes, at times 'The Chief' had been utterly thoughtless and, frequently, feudal in his demands; at others the reverse – thoughtful and considerate. He lived a full and varied life, was much criticized, often justifiably so, but his generosity and kindness far transcended his weaknesses. To me, he will always remain the most noble of noblemen.

12
The End of an Era

The Duke was buried at Eccleston, one of the villages on the Eaton Estate, on the afternoon of 23 July 1953. Present were, of course, the Duchess, family, tenants from the estate, senior members of the staff and the small number within the household who had direct contact with the Duke. A memorial service was to be held at Chester Cathedral the following day and, also, at St Mark's in North Audley Street, London. Whilst Masses were said and paid for by the staff, at Bruree, Lismore and Maynooth.

I flew over from Ireland and stayed with the Ridleys at their house in Eccleston. Over the years we had become close friends, at least so I thought, we had even gone on a holiday together to Majorca in 1952 when – and I appreciate this must be hard to believe – there were only four hotels of any note on the island.

It was a very sombre and sad party that walked back from the church to the Ridley's home that warm summer afternoon, dressed in our morning suits and clutching our top hats, all deep in thought, after the service conducted by the Bishop of Chester. It was the end of an era. George had to leave almost immediately to go to Eaton hall for the reading of the will.

About two hours later he returned, he looked ashen. His wife, Mary, and I asked almost in unison whatever was wrong. We both thought he was ill, for he looked frightful, but he wasn't ill, he was so furious that he could barely speak. The reason – the amount of the legacy the Duke had bequeathed to George. I will not disclose the sum, but it was truly derisory when one considered what he had achieved during his time as chief agent and the millions which would be saved in death duties, and which through his foresight and the ceaseless support of those of us whom he referred to as 'the first eleven', were to become billions. It was not so much the smallness of the bequest that irked, but the lack of appreciation which it, at least to George, represented. That evening, Bill Bryan and his wife, Betty, joined us for dinner. George seemed to have recovered, not from the death of the Duke, but from his hurt over what he took as being lack of gratitude for all his endeavours. He remarked to Bill and me that he would not lessen in any way his efforts to do all he could for the Grosvenors in the course of the battle that he knew lay ahead over death duties. He gave a slight smile and said, "But now I will be in control".

Six weeks later I was summoned to Eaton. A meeting was to take place with the Duchess, Basil Kerr and Ridley, the latter two both being executors of the Duke's will, regarding the future of the Irish estates. After dinner with the Duchess at Eaton Hall, we adjourned to the library, where a table had been prepared in readiness. There was little preamble, in fact it is possible to summarize the Duchess's opening remarks as 'who can we sack and what can we sell in Ireland?' I pointed out that in his Irish will the Duke expressed a wish that all staff and livestock, where possible, should be retained. I remember my horror when she replied, "Ah yes, Mr Twist, a wish not a condition."

George Ridley intervened, saying that the Duke's Irish will was purely academic, for I well knew that the Irish estates had been the Duchess's for many years. On paper that was true, but purely to avoid death duties, a fact I pointed out and that Bryanstown and its 400 plus acres had only been in the Duchess's name five years and eight days, those crucial eight days being sufficient for the property to be free of death duty. I probably did myself no good by pointing out that, for all intents and purposes, they had remained the Duke's. It was he who had to be consulted on any major matters appertaining to the estates, it was he who transferred any money required to the Irish accounts and it was most certainly he to whom telegrams telling of the numerous successes of the herds were sent – never the Duchess. Having passed these comments I again caught a glimpse of the hardness in George's expression that I had noted during our first meeting at Bourdon House. For me it was a miserable evening. The outcome being that I had to return to Ireland, sack fifteen to twenty staff, including Dick Powley, arrange an immediate dispersal sale of the Dairy Shorthorn herd and close the Dublin office.

Very quickly following the Duke's death, George Ridley became the Supremo. His word became law, except over one thing. Once he had firmly established himself in his unassailable position, I, Bill Bryan, John Saunders and Terence Coffee, and I don't know how many others of less seniority, received a letter marked 'Personal' – all were worded in the same way. Briefly, it stated that now he was chairman of the Board of Trustees and senior executor of the Duke's will, he wished in future to be addressed as 'Sir'. I returned my letter in an envelope marked 'Personal', with a hand-written note attached, which simply said, "George, I think this has been sent to me in error, Michael."

We all four compared notes. His cousin, Bill Bryan, returned his with, so he said and I did not doubt him for a second, written diagonally across it the one word 'BALLS'. Terence also returned his with a little note, 'Like Queen Victoria I'm not amused.' John Saunders said he just tore his up and put it in the waste-paper basket. John Saunders was the first to be told his services were no longer required: no thanks, no severance pay, no pension. Not many months later Fort William was put on the market. To my certain knowledge the Duke had spent well over one hundred thousand pounds on the property so that Nancy (the Duchess) should have a lovely home in the part of Ireland he believed she loved. It was sold for a ridiculously low price of £36,000.

I was to learn next that I too had served my purpose and was evicted with just three months' notice. I received the same recognition for all that I had done as John Saunders – not even a thank you.

Next on Ridley's hit list was his cousin, Bill. He, however, was a tougher nut to crack. Like me he had much written evidence of the Duke's dealing in dollars, organized by Ridley. Bill demanded £10,000 severance pay and got it in return for the evidence he had. He upbraided me for not having done the same. Regrettably and probably foolishly, I am not made that way, but at least I still have, safely put away, all the necessary evidence I would have needed had I had similar aspirations as Bill. Terence Coffee on the other hand was in a position not only of personal wealth but a great deal of inside information. Ridley had to accept that the chief accountant was not amused and leave it at that.

Give the devil his due, Ridley worked tirelessly to save the Grosvenor fortune, although some would say he never left himself out of any equation towards this end. In retrospect who could blame him? He'd started by doing the most menial jobs on the Duke's estate and through sheer single-mindedness, total loyalty to the Duke and indifference to the fate of those who had stood by him when they'd served their purpose, he undoubtedly saved the Grosvenor fortune and came to control an empire.

He continued as chairman of the trustees until 1972, aided by Geoffrey Singer and Tom Barty-King, together with a host of other helpers. He achieved remarkable success. Death duties, I was given to understand, were eventually agreed at an unbelievably low figure of just over £19 million.

There are now over one hundred factories on Annacis Island. The Grosvenors no longer count their money in millions, but, if the media are to be believed, they do so in billions. Whilst their wealth is spread around the whole country, and in many parts of the world, the hub from which the majority of their wealth emanated was when in the latter part of the seventeenth century Sir Thomas Grosvenor married Mary Davies, who had inherited the Ebury manor from her father, Alexander Davies. The Ebury Estate bordered the outermost areas of London, it also adjoined Millbank, which was owned by the Grosvenors, and extended from Marble Arch to the Thames. In the years that followed it was to be developed into Belgravia, Mayfair, Berkeley Square and the not quite so fashionable Pimlico.

Halfway up the main stairs at Bourdon House hung a portrait of Mary Davies. It was not unknown for the Duke, when in a mellow mood heading for bed, to stop on the half-landing, turn to the painting, give a little bow and say, "Thank you, my dear." Perhaps some future Grosvenor will enact the same ritual to a photograph of George Ridley, but somehow I doubt it.

About Farming Books and Videos Ltd.

Farming Books and Videos Ltd is a small family-run business that offers a wide range of publications for the farmer, smallholder and country dweller.

For further information or to request an up-to-date catalogue please contact:-

Farming Books and Videos Ltd.
PO Box 536
Preston
PR2 9ZY
Tel 01772 652693
info@farmingbooksandvideos.com

www.farmingbooksandvideos.com

Also by Michael Twist

The Spacious Days
ISBN 0-9542555-8-5
This personal account of growing up on an estate at Burnham in Buckinghamshire in the 1920s and 30s, recalls an age of agriculture with a large labour force, where there was time to do a job well and time to talk, chaff, and enjoy a bit of shooting. These are real stories of real people from a long-gone age where man worked in harmony with nature.

Hallowed Acres
ISBN 0-904871-00-3
In tandem with *The Spacious Days*, this second volume of Michael Twist's reminiscences is full of humour in its depiction of the characters on the Burnham estate and the experiences of a young lad growing into manhood. It tells of the wildlife that abounded throughout the country, of his friendship with a family of true Romany gypsies, of country pastimes and of eagerly awaited agricultural shows and competitions.

The Glory Days
ISBN 0-904871-01-1
The third book in Michael Twist's evocative rural autobiography recalls one of the great ages of farming and a time when farmers were truly appreciated – during the Second World War. Invalided out of the army, the author becomes estate manager on the run-down Roundhill Estate in the Vale of Aylesbury. Challenges include restructuring the labour force with the aid of Land Girls, building up a herd of top Dairy Shorthorns, as well as helping the country's war effort.

'Michael Twist's books are essential reading for agricultural and sociology students.'
www.countrysportsandcountrylife.com

'Michael Twist's books all capture a wonderful way of life in the country that has now ceased to be.' The *Limerick Leader*

Other Titles Available

You've Done What, My Lord?
By Rory Clark
ISBN 09542555-1-8

When James Aden applies for the position of Deputy Agent at Rumshott, one of the finest landed estates in England, he little realizes what he has let himself in for. Negotiating with royalty, tenant farmers, lost parrots, escaping sheep and the imperious Lady Leghorn all appear to be part of the job description. This is a highly acclaimed first novel by a former land agent is based on his experiences working for some of the largest estates in Britain.

An English Country Manner
By Rory Clark
ISBN 0-9542555-0-X

When tragic circumstances force James Aden to leave Scotland he eventually finds a new job as the agent on Sir Charles Buckley's vast Suffolk estate. Once again he has to deal with an unusual list of problems. Rogue chimney pots, unsavoury tenants and delinquent sheep are just some of his responsibilities. Much awaited sequel to Rory Clark's popular novel, *You've Done What, My Lord?*

All in a Day's Work
Patricia Warren
ISBN 0-9542555-9-3
Borrowing £50 from the farm accounts, farmer's wife Patricia Warren set up the very first lonely hearts introduction agency for farmers. Her aim was to introduce couples with the hope that their friendships would develop into long term relationships or marriage.

Some twenty years and countless couples later Patricia has written a book charting the rise of the Farmers and Country Bureau and some of the characters and stories she has encountered along the way, in a highly entertaining book.